Watercolour
Landscapes

Watercolour
Landscapes
Projects, Tips and Techniques

General Editor: Richard Taylor

amber
BOOKS

First published in 2006 by
Amber Books Ltd
Bradley's Close
74-77 White Lion Street
London N1 9PF
www.amberbooks.co.uk

ISBN-13: 978-1-904687-71-9
ISBN-10: 1-904687-71-7

Distributed in the UK by
Bookmart Ltd
Blaby Road
Wigston
Leicester LE18 4SE

Contributing Artists:
Joe Dowden 6-13, 22-28, 29-35, 56-62; Abi Edgar: 69-75;
Shirley Felts: 76-83; Bill Newton: 14-21; William Newton: 90-96;
Kay Ohsten: 36-41, 84-89; John Palmer: 49-55; Jane Telford: 42-48;
Paula Velarde: 65-68

Picture Credits:
All DeAgostini/George Taylor except the following: Corbis 36t;
DeAgostini/Shona Wood: 69-75

Printed in Singapore

Contents

Looking out over the valley

Warm and cool watercolours are used together to convey vast distances in this magnificent view from a hilltop.

We are all familiar with the great thrill that panoramic views from the top of a hill afford, and this watercolour painting certainly captures that feeling. One's emotional reaction when viewing a scene for the first time – the 'first seduction' – is an important element of any painting, and your aim should be to invite your viewers

▼ **The high viewpoint and strong curve of the path create an exciting composition in this scene. The eye tumbles into the valley then lingers over the series of thin, colourful fields in the distance.**

to share that vision. Once a scene takes your fancy, assess whether or not it will make a good painting by looking at how you can turn it into a good composition.

Inviting composition

A landscape subject should have an entrance point and a destination. Try to design your composition in a way that invites the viewer to journey into the painting and roam around a little. In this painting, the rough track on the left is the directional force that carries the eye through the scene. Take note, however, that the path is not too dominant – it is

FIRST STEPS

1 ▼ **Sketch the composition** Using an HB pencil, sketch out the bare bones of the landscape – include the trees, path and horizon. Here, the artist drew on to a sheet of tracing paper first, then traced off the lines – this is less obtrusive than drawing directly on to the paper.

interrupted by other elements such as trees and the curved line of the hill.

Colour recession

In a scene such as this, the range of tones and colours – from the nearest to the farthest – must be accurately assessed in terms of strength. If one is either too strong or too weak, the impression of a gradual recession will be destroyed. For instance, a field of oilseed rape might be a vivid yellow, but if it is in the distance it will appear to 'jump out' if you do not pay attention to how recession diminishes the intensity of the colour.

2 ◄ **Work on the foreground track** Draw the stones strewn across the dirt track, making them smaller in the distance. Using a colour shaper, (see Trouble Shooter on next page) mask them out with masking fluid. To represent the smallest stones, spatter some masking fluid flicked from an old toothbrush. Then apply more to the trunks and branches of the silver birch trees with the colour shaper.

BRUSH SAVER

Save wear and tear on your watercolour brushes by using a colour shaper (a type of brush with a flexible rubber tip instead of hairs) to apply the masking fluid. Even dried-on fluid is easy to remove by peeling it off the rubber tip.

3 ▲ **Apply colour to the sky** Use a No. 30 squirrel mop to wet the entire paper with clean water. Change to a No. 10 round brush and apply a narrow band of rose madder across the horizon line. Allow the colour to drift up into the sky and below the horizon. Then apply a band of yellow ochre across the top of the picture and let it merge into the pink area.

5 ▼ **Darken the sky** Rinse the No. 10 round brush in clean water and wet the sky area. Then sweep in streaks of grey-violet mixed from ultramarine warmed with a tiny drop of alizarin crimson. Add more ultramarine to the mix to make it bluer and paint a darker streak along the horizon.

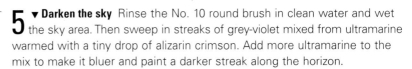

4 ▲ **Underpaint the foreground** Make a fairly strong wash of cadmium yellow and work it over the foreground with broad, sweeping strokes of the No. 30 mop brush. Vary the tone with a few strokes of burnt sienna applied wet-on-wet. Allow to dry.

6 ▼ **Create clouds** While the sky wash is still wet, lift out cumulus clouds at the top with a small wad of tissue. Avoid rubbing, as this will spoil the surface of the paper; use a quick, press-and-lift motion. Lift out streaks of flat cloud with the 'edge' of the tissue wad.

7 ▲ **Develop the clouds** Tilt your board downwards and soften the undersides of the clouds by 'tickling' them with a clean, damp brush. Then put in some dark clouds with small, rapid movements of the brush, using the same grey-violet mix as before, but darkened with more ultramarine.

DEVELOPING THE PICTURE

The foreground, middle ground and background are now established as simple shapes. Start to develop the landscape features and the effects of aerial perspective. As you do this, remember to keep the whole composition in mind, rather than concentrating on individual parts.

8 ▶ **Start painting the foreground bushes** Rinse the brush clean and shake off the excess water. Scrub the damp brush lightly over the right-hand corner of the painting, working it in different directions. Quickly dry-brush over these wet strokes with a mix of cadmium yellow and burnt sienna.

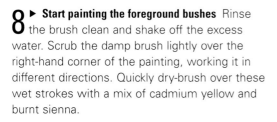

9 ▶ Establish the foreground and middle ground Use the same method as in step 8 to establish the sloping line of trees in the middle distance, behind the birch trees. Now darken the mix with a touch of ultramarine and scuff the shadows on the dirt track, again using water first so that the strokes are softened.

10 ▼ Add detail Suggest grass below the trees with a dilute mixture of cadmium yellow and phthalo green. Darken the mixture with more phthalo green and paint the grass in the foreground with quick dry-brush strokes interspersed with brown shadows mixed from burnt sienna and ultramarine. Put in shadows cast by the stones, using the No. 10 round for big ones and a No. 2 round for small ones.

11 ▼ Introduce mid tones Pick up a small amount of burnt sienna on the No. 10 brush and apply loose, scrubby strokes over the trees in the middle distance and the bushes in the foreground on the right. Mix burnt sienna and ultramarine, and suggest the cool, dark shadows between the trees with small, quick strokes of the No. 2 brush.

12 ▶ Put in distant fields Continue with the same mix for the shadows in the foreground bushes, applying the paint with upward flicks of the brush. Changing to the No. 10 round, paint the distant, bright yellow cornfield with a continuous stroke of cadmium yellow (dampen the area with clean water first). Mix in some burnt sienna and paint the field beyond the cornfield with a narrow band of colour. Add a little rose madder for the farthest fields, leaving small flashes of white paper between them.

13 ▶ Continue with the background Darken the wooded area in front of the cornfield with loose, wet-on-wet strokes of burnt sienna overlaid with touches of cadmium yellow. Start to put in the distant fields with thin streaks of phthalo green. Mix ultramarine with a hint of phthalo blue (for intensity) and alizarin crimson (for warmth), and put in the line of blue hills on the horizon, using the very tip of the brush.

14 ▼ Add more detail Use the same blue mix to suggest lines of trees and hedgerows in the distance, working over some of the undercolours. The yellow undercolour will show through, making a green. Use bigger strokes for the trees in front of the cornfield to show that they are nearer.

15 ▶ Paint treetops on the right Dip the No. 10 brush in clean water, squeeze out the excess and loosely work over the middle ground on the right of the picture. Go over the area with loose strokes of Van Dyke brown and ultramarine, letting the colours run and blend on the damp paper to give an impression of treetops in hazy light. Introduce strokes of burnt sienna and cadmium yellow in the same way.

Express yourself
Nature distilled

In this version of the landscape, the elements are pared down to interlocking shapes of warm and cool colour. The paper was first wetted and broad sweeps of colour were applied with a large, soft brush, leaving flecks of white paper to offset the intense colours. Despite the lack of recognizable detail, these contrasting shapes and colours read as a landscape receding into the distance.

16 ▼ **Increase recession** Using the dampened No. 30 mop, lightly sweep over the fields to soften them. Mute the colour of the cornfield with a mix of cadmium yellow and yellow ochre. With the No. 10 brush and clean water, lift out a streak of colour from the green field, then apply cadmium yellow to suggest sunlight. Draw bands of the blue mix from step 13 across the yellow field.

17 ▶ **Paint the cast shadows** Mix a dilute wash of cerulean blue and burnt sienna and use this to suggest the rutted surface of the dirt track with quick dry-brush strokes worked in different directions. Paint more dark shadows cast by the nearby trees with an intense dark mixed from Van Dyke brown and ultramarine.

18 ▼ **Paint the twigs** Dip the tip of the No. 10 round in water, shake off the excess and paint the twigs of the birches with rapid dry-brush strokes. Then dip the brush into the dark brown wash and go over the strokes again with the brush held perpendicular. Skip it over the surface to create thick to thin calligraphic marks.

19 ◀ **Paint the birch trees** Remove the masking fluid from the birches. Mix a greenish yellow from yellow ochre, burnt sienna and a touch of phthalo green. Wet the tree trunks with clean water, then add the colour to the left edge of the trunk and let it drift across the damp paper. While this is damp, paint shadows on the trunks with Van Dyke brown and a little ultramarine. Again, touch the brush to the edge and let the colour drift.

20 ◀ **Paint the stones** Finish painting the birch trees, leaving flecks of white paper on the branches to suggest light reflecting off the silvery bark. Remove the masking fluid from the stones in the foreground. Lightly touch each stone with water, then apply a mix of cerulean blue and yellow ochre, leaving tiny flecks of white paper here and there. Just before they dry, touch in some shadows and cracks on the nearest stones with the dark brown mix.

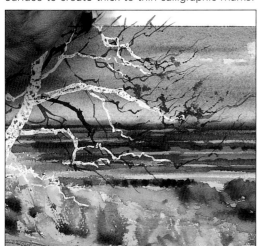

A FEW STEPS FURTHER

There is plenty for the eye to explore in the open spaces of this atmospheric landscape. A hint of scratching out will add a final touch of subtle texture.

21 ▶ **Use sgraffito** With the tip of a sharp craft knife blade, scratch out a few fine, broken lines that suggest light catching the branches of young saplings in the middle distance.

22 ▲ **Add shadows** Paint the shadow sides of the saplings with the dark brown mix from step 17, using the very tip of the No. 10 round to produce fine lines.

THE FINISHED PICTURE

A Depth and distance
Cool, recessive blues and greens in the distance contrast with warm golds in the foreground, a device that emphasizes the effects of aerial perspective.

B Breaking the boundaries
The birch trees break the frame at the top, bringing them forward in the picture plane and pushing the landscape back into the distance by contrast.

C Counterbalance
The bushes at bottom right counterbalance the birch trees at top left, giving the composition equilibrium and forming a 'frame' for the landscape beyond.

Sailing barges

A vast expanse of sky provides a luminous backdrop to traditional sailing barges with their jumble of masts, furled sails and rigging.

Harbours and estuaries are a rich source of painting material and are often more interesting when the tide is out. At low tide there are pools of water with reflections in them, boats tilted on their sides and an assortment of mooring ropes and buoys.

Rather than attempt to take in an entire scene, try to find a small area that catches your eye. Feel free to move objects around to achieve a better composition. Here, the artist felt that the jetty on the left was too obtrusive, so he pushed it back and made it smaller. He added extra elements on the right to balance the weight of the boats on the left.

Using a rigger brush

Rather than labouring over the barges' rigging, suggest it simply with slightly broken lines. This is where a rigger brush comes in handy. It has very long, flexible hair and the extra-fine point enables you to make hairline strokes. In fact, the name 'rigger' goes back to the days of big sailing ships, when painters of seascapes used this type of brush to render the complex rigging accurately.

▼ **In this evocative marine view, the artist combines close observation of the subject with economy of detail.**

YOU WILL NEED

Piece of 300gsm
(140lb) NOT
watercolour paper
30.5 x 40.5cm
(12 x 16in)

4B pencil

8 watercolours: raw
sienna; ultramarine;
light red; cadmium
red; lemon yellow;
burnt sienna;
cobalt blue; brown
madder alizarin

Brushes: 25mm (1in)
flat; Nos. 6, 14 and 4
rounds; No. 1 rigger

Mixing palette
or dish

Jar of water

Ruler

FIRST STEPS

1 ▶ Start with a drawing
Make a light pencil outline drawing of the scene. Position the horizon line low down on the page so as to give full emphasis to the boats and their tall masts. Pay attention to shapes, angles and proportions, but don't get bogged down with every last detail.

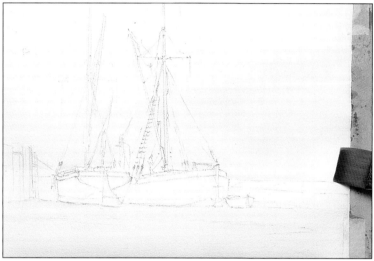

2 ◀ Apply a background wash
Working with the 25mm (1in) flat brush, dampen the entire paper except for the boat hulls. Block in the sky and the foreground with a thin, transparent wash of raw sienna watercolour to give a warm tone overall.

3 ▼ Paint the clouds Just before the underwash dries, mix a dilute wash of ultramarine and make soft, diagonal strokes in the upper left of the sky with the flat brush. Put in the storm cloud at top right with a stronger wash, then sweep the brush down and across, letting the colour fade out. While the ultramarine is still damp, float a hint of light red into the lower clouds to give them a warm tint.

4 ▲ Define the horizon Make a dilute mix of ultramarine and a little cadmium red. Still using the flat brush, suggest a reddening sky by sweeping in a band of this soft mauve shade across the horizon line.

5 ▼ Paint the water Mix a muted green from ultramarine with a little lemon yellow and raw sienna and, using a No. 6 round brush, put in the line of trees in the far distance. Switch to a No. 14 round brush and put in the pools of water in the foreground with very dilute ultramarine.

6 ▲ Paint the mud banks Now put in the mud banks with sweeping strokes of raw sienna. While these are still damp, float on darker patches of mud with a brownish mix of light red and ultramarine, letting them settle softly into the underwash. Make a stronger version of the same mix and use the tip of the brush to make broken lines, suggesting ridges in the mud.

7 ◄ Add background details Mix varied mid tones of green and grey from ultramarine and raw sienna. Give the distant trees and mud banks a little more definition with tiny marks made with the tip of the No. 6 round brush.

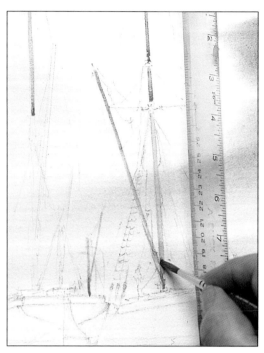

DEVELOPING THE PICTURE

Now that the sky and background are established, you can turn your attention to the boats. These are the focus of the painting, but try to integrate them naturally with the surrounding sea and sky by avoiding too many details and hard edges.

8 ▲ Paint the jetty Mix raw sienna, ultramarine and light red in varied proportions and paint the wooden jetty with vertical strokes of a No. 4 round brush. Keep these washes light and broken – the jetty is right on the edge of the picture and, if you overstate it, it will draw the eye and unbalance the composition.

9 ▲ Paint the masts Mix a warm brown from raw sienna and burnt sienna, dilute it well and begin painting the wooden masts with the No. 6 brush. To steady your hand, hold a ruler at an angle and rest the ferrule of the brush against its edge. Vary the tones of brown, and make the upper parts of the masts slightly darker where they are silhouetted against the light sky.

10 ◄ Start on the hulls Fill in the back panel of the left-hand boat with a pale wash of cobalt blue. Mix a strong blue-black from ultramarine and light red, and paint the hull of the right-hand boat, leaving slivers of white paper showing to define its form.

11

▼ **Complete one of the hulls** Mix raw sienna and light red, and paint the base of the right-hand hull, letting this colour bleed into the darker one above. Rinse the brush, shake out the excess water and lift out some colour to show where the hull curves towards the prow and reflects more light.

12

▲ **Complete the other hull** Paint the hull and rudder of the left-hand boat, using the same colour mixes as in steps 10 and 11, but this time making them slightly darker in tone, particularly where the back of the hull curves under. Again, leave slivers of white paper to help define the shapes.

EXPERT ADVICE
Soft focus

Although boats are solid structures, avoid using dense tones and hard edges when you paint them. In a watercolour painting, boats should harmonize with the surrounding elements of sky and water. Use a damp brush to soften the line where one colour or tone meets another, and where the bottom of the boat meets the water or the mud bank on which it is resting.

13

▲ **Paint the sails** Use light red to put in the red trim on the little dinghy on the right. Then mix a rich brown from brown madder alizarin and raw sienna, and start painting the furled sails.

14 ▼ **Put in the rigging** Mix a dark wash of ultramarine and light red, and use the No. 1 rigger brush to put in the crosstree and ropes that make up the rigging on the right-hand boat. Use a ruler to steady your hand, but try not to make the lines too rigid. Keep the brush fairly dry, use a very light touch and vary the weight of the lines.

16 ▼ **Paint reflections** Mix a greenish-grey from ultramarine and raw sienna, and, using the No. 14 brush, paint the reflections of the boats and wooden pilings in the foreground water. Make sure each reflection sits directly beneath the object reflecting it. Add a touch more ultramarine for the darker reflections, painting them with vertical strokes while the paint is still damp so that they blend softly together.

15 ▲ **Complete the rigging** Paint the rigging on the left-hand boat in the same way. Suggest hatches and other deck details with a muted green mix of lemon yellow and ultramarine.

A FEW STEPS FURTHER

Step back from the picture and assess what is needed to complete it. Some cast shadows will strengthen the forms, and some small details on the right will give the composition better balance.

17 ▲ **Add the mooring pile** Mix a grey-brown from ultramarine and light red, and paint the mooring pile on the right with a dry No. 4 brush – its top extends above the horizon to add to the feeling of depth. Paint its reflection in the pool with broken lines in a slightly lighter tone.

Express yourself

Getting proportions right

In this rapidly executed sketch, made with a dip pen and ink, the artist focuses on capturing the 'personality' of a small fishing vessel. All boats have their own character, conveyed by the shapes of their hulls, masts and sails. However quickly and simply you draw them, it is vital to get their basic proportions right. Start by comparing the length of a boat to the height of its mast. Then check, for example, the length of the cabin against the length of the deck, and so on.

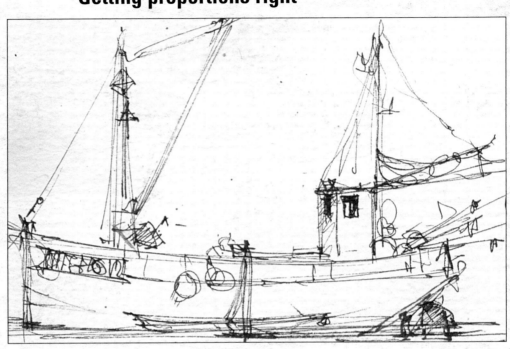

18 ▼ Add shadows Dampen the No. 14 brush and run it along the bottom of the boats to soften the line where boat and sand meet. Using darker versions of the mixes from step 8, strengthen the jetty and put in the shadows it casts on the sand. Paint the shadow on the right-hand boat with a fairly dark mix of ultramarine and light red.

19 ▲ Work on the sails Mix brown madder alizarin with a touch of ultramarine, and, with the tip of the No. 6 brush, put in the dark shadows and folds on the sails.

20 ▼ **Add foreground detail** With the rigger brush and a mix of ultramarine and brown madder alizarin, suggest the mooring lines tying the boats to the mooring pile and lying on the foreshore. Use a deft, light touch, letting the lines break up.

21 ▲ **Add some seagulls** Use the tip of the No. 6 round brush and the same dark mix to enliven the sky area with seagulls. Be sparing – scattering too many little 'V-shapes' everywhere can ruin a perfectly good painting. Include small groups as well as single birds, and vary their size, tone and wing positions.

THE FINISHED PICTURE

A Tall masts
Taking the tall masts of the barges right off the top of the picture area emphasizes their height and gives the viewer the feeling of being close to the subject.

B Lead-ins
The sweeping diagonal shape of the blue cloud leads the eye down to the centre of interest – the two sailing barges.

C Watch the birdie
Seagulls wheeling overhead on the right complement the bulk of the boats on the left, add detail to the wide expanse of sky and animate the scene.

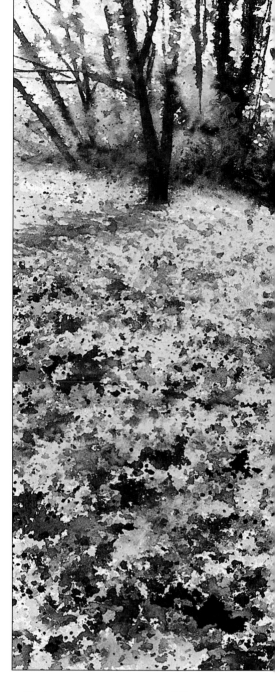

Riverbank reflections

Various watercolour techniques are used to great effect in this painting of a cool, shady stretch of river, with the sun filtering through the trees.

There are three main elements found in this lovely river scene – water, grass and trees. Each element is treated separately and each is painted using a different technique. This jigsaw approach will enable you to complete the painting in simplified stages, and you will have the satisfaction of seeing how the pieces eventually fit together to make a realistic landscape.

Start by making the initial drawing on tracing paper. In this way you can experiment with the composition without spoiling the paper. The transferred image will always be clean and minimal – an ideal start for watercolour painting.

Grass and foliage

Spattering is the key to the fresh, grassy banks – first with clean water, then with colour, so that the paint finds its way into the wet shapes. The first spatter of colour looks like an explosion of tiny stars, but as the sequence is repeated the 'stars' eventually build up to form a perfect impression of grass and leaves.

To create perspective in the painting, make the foreground spatters larger than those in the background by spattering with the brush held closer to the paper.

Watery reflections

Paradoxically, the fluid nature of water is most effectively painted with precise brush strokes. Here, both vertical and horizontal strokes are used to create the reflections in the river. Paint the reflections wet-on-wet; when dry, they provide a soft background for more precise ripples and reflected shapes, overpainted in stronger colours.

▲ **Lively spattered texture on the foliage contrasts with the glassy surface of the river in this peaceful scene.**

YOU WILL NEED

Piece of 400gsm (200lb) NOT watercolour paper 38 x 51cm (15 x 20in)

Tracing paper (size as above)

B pencil

Masking fluid; old toothbrush and paint brush (to apply masking fluid)

Scraps of paper to mask painting

Brushes: Nos. 6 and 4 rounds; fan blender; No. 1 rigger or fine liner

Woodcock feather (optional)

10 watercolours: cadmium lemon; phthalo green; turquoise light; indigo; burnt sienna; alizarin crimson; Naples yellow; Payne's grey; ultramarine; cerulean blue

Gum arabic; paper tissue

FIRST STEPS

1 ▼ **Trace the image** Having sketched the image on to tracing paper, draw with a B pencil over the main lines on the reverse of the paper.

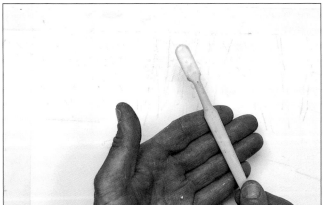

2 ▲ **Apply masking fluid** Transfer the image on to watercolour paper by turning the tracing paper the right way up and going over the lines with a sharp pencil. Use an old paint brush to dab masking fluid between the trees. Also mask distant horizontal reflections and the stumps in the foreground. Use an old toothbrush to spatter masking fluid across the background.

3 ▼ **Block in the river bank** Mask off the river with scrap paper. Using a No. 6 round brush, spatter water on to the grassy bank on the left. Dab on cadmium lemon, allowing the colour to run into the blobs of water. At the top, blend the yellow with more water to create a wash of solid colour.

4 ▲ **Continue blocking in** Wet the right-hand bank and flood the area with cadmium lemon, leaving a broad band of white along the top of the picture.

Express yourself

Down the road

Here is another watercolour, painted with many of the same techniques as the step-by-step. Here, however, the river is replaced by a road. Note how the blues and purples of the wet tarmac surface contrast with the yellows and greens of the verge. The long, linear tree shadows across the road also make a pleasing contrast with the spattered detail on the verge.

5 ▼ **Suggest the grass** Mask out all the areas around the right-hand bank. Mix phthalo green and cadmium lemon, and flick the mixture on to the wet cadmium lemon paint.

6 ▲ **Suggest the background** To suggest the distant trees on the right, lightly apply water to the paper, then spatter and dab the wet area with varying mixtures of cadmium lemon, turquoise light, indigo, burnt sienna and alizarin crimson. Allow the colours to run together on the wet paper.

7 ▼ **Continue the background** Paint the tree-trunks and branches in cadmium lemon. Moving to the left, lightly wet the paper, spatter on turquoise light and phthalo green paint, then blend the colours in the shady areas around the base of the trees.

DEVELOPING THE PICTURE

The main areas of grass and foliage have been initially blocked in with yellow and green, and it is time to start work on the trees. There is a handy technique for painting them quickly and effectively.

8 ▶ **Paint the trees** Change to a No. 4 round and paint green bands across one of the tree trunks in a dilute mix of indigo, turquoise light and Naples yellow. Define the trunk by dragging Payne's grey quickly down through the wet bands. The paint will run horizontally to suggest branches.

**EXPERT ADVICE
Fine lines with a feather**

In the nineteenth century, marine artists and architects often used a tail feather of a woodcock to paint fine, even lines. The feather, which is very springy and holds a surprising amount of colour, is used here taped to a brush handle to paint the long, thin branches of the trees. If you do not have a woodcock feather to hand, a No. 1 rigger or fine liner brush does a similar job.

9 ▲ **Develop the grass** With the No. 6 brush, develop the far bank, alternately spattering it with water and then with a mixture of phthalo green and indigo to create the light and dark greens. Use the tip of the brush to take the colour up to the edge of the water.

10 ▼ **Complete the trees** Use the No. 4 brush and burnt sienna to paint the bank of trees on the right-hand side. But don't overdo it – work from the wrist to achieve natural curves on trunks and branches.

11 ▼ **Build up the grass tones** Moving to the left bank, spatter the grass with drops of water, then with dilute phthalo green. Repeat to build up textured colour, adding indigo for the darker foreground tones.

12 ▼ **Paint the water** Using the No. 6 brush, block in the river in broad, horizontal strokes of ultramarine. Use deep colour in the foreground, diluting it as you move towards the distance. While the colour is wet, smooth out brush marks with water and a fan blender.

13 ▼ **Suggest reflections** Start to paint the foreground reflections into the wet blue paint, applying mixes of burnt sienna and indigo with vertical and horizontal strokes.

14 ▲ **Add distant reflections** Wet the far part of the river with water mixed with gum arabic. Using the No.4 round, work over this with vertical strokes of Naples yellow. Add darker bands with mixes of cadmium lemon, Payne's grey and burnt sienna.

15 ▲ **Remove masking fluid** Paint strokes of indigo mixed with burnt sienna between the bands of masking fluid on the water. Leave the painting to dry; rub off the masking fluid from the background and water. Paint a dilute mix of indigo, burnt sienna and phthalo green among the trees; add reflections in a mix of phthalo green, indigo and burnt sienna.

A FEW STEPS FURTHER

The picture is almost complete, but more can be made of the ripples and reflections on the river. So far, these are suggested with soft, wet-on-wet brush strokes. Now allow the painting to dry completely, so that you can add some crisper reflections to the surface of the water.

16 ▶ **Paint moving water** With the No. 6 brush, paint the reflections of the trees in the foreground in a dark mixture of indigo, burnt sienna and phthalo green, adding touches of lemon yellow for the paler tones. Use squiggly, tapering lines to capture the movement of the water.

17 ▲ **Define the bank** Continue building up reflections, diluting the mix to make lighter tones. Use the No. 4 brush for finer lines. Apply water along the edge of the river bank and flood with mixes of cerulean blue, turquoise light and cadmium yellow.

18 ▼ **Add branches** Paint the reflections of the fine branches in mixes of indigo, burnt sienna and phthalo green. Our artist used a woodcock feather for the tapering lines, but a No. 1 rigger or fine liner brush works well, too. Apply water across the far ripples, then dab off some of the colour with a paper tissue.

19 ▲ **Paint the posts** Remove the masking fluid from the wooden posts and paint the tops in a mix of burnt sienna and cadmium lemon with the No. 4 brush. Add the shadow in indigo mixed with burnt sienna.

THE FINISHED PICTURE

A Background sunlight
White sunlight filtering through the trees is established in the early stages of the painting with masking fluid.

B Grass and foliage
The river bank is built up by spattering the paper with water and paint alternately to achieve a mottled, leafy texture.

C Wavy lines
The moving surface of the water is created by using horizontal lines with squiggly and zigzag marks.

Rocks and masonry

Capture the massive solidity of a craggy cliff and the textures of aged, flaking plaster and weathered masonry in two watercolour projects.

M ost landscape subjects include some hard surfaces in the form of outcrops of rock or man-made features such as buildings or bridges. To create landscape paintings that are accurate, varied and interesting, it is important to describe these features as effectively as more fluid forms such as trees, bushes and grass.

In this project, two different 'hard' subjects are painted in watercolour. The first (above) shows a spectacular view of buildings perched on top of a sheer cliff of stratified rock. The subject of the second one is an old weathered barn with broken rendering exposing the stonework. Various watercolour techniques have been used to bring out the characteristics of the hard surfaces.

Looking and sketching

In order to paint rock features or buildings in the landscape effectively, spend time observing and sketching them. Make studies of natural and man-made structures, either outdoors or from reference photographs. In rugged landscapes, look at how the rock is

▲ **The stratified formation of this towering cliff is captured very simply, using layered washes and horizontal brush strokes.**

formed. Compare the appearance of bands of rock with that of hard granite outcrops or chalk cliffs. Become familiar, too, with the character of building materials – the smoothness of a rendered wall, the crumbling character of weathered stucco, the regularity of brick.

Note how distance and the play of light affect the appearance of hard surfaces. Standing close to a brick building, for example, you can see the grainy texture and subtle tonal variations of individual bricks, and the contrasting texture of the lines of mortar. Further away you can make out a regular pattern and an overall colour, while further away still you can see only an overall shape and a generalized colour.

The quality of the light and the angle of the sun also affect what you can see.

On a grey day, textures appear flattened, while, on a sunny one, contrasts of light and shadow allow you to see quite small surface details.

Rendering what you see

Close observation is only part of the story. You also need to consider which techniques are best suited to representing what you see. It isn't necessary to render every last detail. Try to find a shorthand

mark that suggests the material at the distance from which it is being viewed – use it here and there, but make sure that you do not overdo it.

If you give the eye enough clues, it will fill in the details. A few areas of dashes will be enough to suggest that a wall is constructed from brick, while some horizontal lines and dry-brushed marks will tell viewers that they are looking at bands of rock.

PROJECT 1

SHEER CLIFF AND BUILDINGS

A simple approach is best for this spectacular subject. Use layered washes to capture the warm honey tones and rugged qualities of the rock. Depict the different layers with horizontal brush strokes and add the vertical cracks wet-on-dry in the final stages, using the very tip of the brush.

YOU WILL NEED

Piece of 300gsm (140lb) NOT watercolour paper 30 x 36cm (12 x 14in)

2B pencil

Brushes: Nos. 8, 4 and 3 rounds

12 watercolours: cobalt blue; yellow ochre; Alizarin crimson; indigo; cadmium yellow; cerulean blue; burnt sienna; Naples yellow; raw umber; phthalo blue; ivory black; ultramarine

Scrap paper

FIRST STEPS

1 ▶ Lay in the underpainting Map out the subject using a 2B pencil. Mix a wash of cobalt blue, yellow ochre and alizarin crimson, and, with a No. 8 round brush, apply over the scene – reserve the white paper for highlights on the cliff. Paint a wash of indigo wet-on-wet over the landscape on the left.

2 ◀ Apply colour to the rock face Flood alizarin crimson and cadmium yellow into the landscape on the left. Mix a large wash of yellow ochre and use a No. 4 round brush to work the paint over the still-wet cliff face. Allow to dry.

3 ▼ **Build up the background** Now apply the cobalt blue, yellow ochre and alizarin crimson wash from step 1 to the background, using the No. 8 brush. Take the wash carefully along the silhouette of the cliff to sharpen it up.

DEVELOPING THE PICTURE

You can now start to capture the unique character of the rock by using layered washes applied wet-on-dry. Allow the painting to dry between washes.

5 ▲ **Develop the cliff** Use the No. 4 round and a mix of Naples yellow and burnt sienna on the left of the cliff. Leave to dry; add more burnt sienna to the mix and use this towards the base of the cliff.

EXPERT ADVICE
Tone matching

To check the exact tone and hue of an area of your photo, you need to view it in isolation. Cut a small hole in a sheet of paper and place it over the area – it is much easier to assess the tone when it is surrounded by white. Lay a patch of your paint mix alongside it to check its accuracy.

4 ▼ **Apply tone to the buildings** Mix cerulean blue and burnt sienna, and apply this dark mix over the buildings perched on top of the cliff. Use the tip of the brush to define their silhouettes.

6 ▲ **Add detail and vegetation** Drag raw umber into the horizontal and vertical bands on the right of the cliff to suggest layers and cracks in the rock. Add strokes of burnt sienna and a burnt sienna/Naples yellow mix on the left. Paint bushes at the top of the cliff with a wash of cobalt and indigo, then add a mix of alizarin crimson, phthalo blue and ivory black wet-on-wet, with a No. 3 round brush.

7 ▶ Work on the buildings
Use ultramarine and burnt sienna for the roofs of the buildings and for the shadowy windows. Differentiate the arched and straight tops of the windows, but don't work too precisely – the details should be in keeping with the degree of precision in the rest of the painting.

8 ◀ Add rock strata
Make sure the painting is dry. Tear a sheet of scrap paper and use the torn edge to mask the left edge of the projecting outcrop on the right. Mix ultramarine and burnt sienna, then apply horizontal strokes with the tip of the No. 8 round to indicate the layers in the rock, taking the brush marks over the mask.

9 ▲ Paint in final details Use the tip of the No. 3 round brush and a dark mix of ultramarine, burnt sienna and ivory black to apply details such as the thin vertical fissures and cracks in the rock face.

THE FINISHED PICTURE

A Simplified detail
The architectural details were rendered very simply, so as not to distract the viewer's attention from the main subject of the painting – the cliff face.

B Sunlit edge
The white of the paper was left to stand for the light area on the edge of the cliff, where it catches the full force of the sun.

C Layered washes
Layers of transparent washes applied wet-on-wet and wet-on-dry capture the complex textures of the honey and grey tones on the rock face.

PROJECT 2

OLD BARN

Capture the flaking stucco and weathered masonry of this old barn, using a combination of wax resist, masking and layered washes of watercolour. Before you begin painting, mask off the edges of the picture area with tape – this will give a crisp outline to the finished work.

FIRST STEPS

1 ▼ Mask the stucco Using a 2B pencil, sketch the main elements. Apply masking fluid to the outline of the white plaster with the tip of a paint shaper. Mask the top half of the window bars.

YOU WILL NEED

Piece of 300gsm (140lb) NOT watercolour paper 33 x 25cm (13 x 10in)

Masking tape

2B pencil

Paint shaper and masking fluid

Brushes: Nos. 8 and 4 rounds

9 watercolours: ultramarine; yellow ochre; alizarin crimson; Payne's grey; burnt sienna; ivory black; Naples yellow; cobalt blue; lemon yellow

Kitchen paper

White candle

2 ◄ Apply the sky Apply a wash of ultramarine to the sky with a No. 8 round brush. Roll kitchen paper into a cylinder and dab it in the wet wash to create a variety of cloud effects.

3 ▼ Paint the masonry Mix a wash of yellow ochre and grey it slightly with touches of alizarin crimson and ultramarine to make a buff shade. Using the No. 8 round brush, wash this colour over the masonry. Leave to dry.

DEVELOPING THE PICTURE

The main elements – the sky, the stucco and the stonework – are now broadly established. Begin to create the textures of the stonework by applying linear detail, wax resist and layers of wash.

4 ► Add the dark tones The shadows cast by the projecting stones allow you to see the construction of the wall. Using the tip of a No. 4 round brush and a wash of Payne's grey, draw the horizontal lines of shadows between the stones. The ragged edge of the stucco also casts a shadow, so trace this with the tip of the brush. Leave to dry.

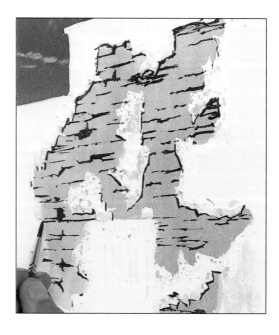

33

5 ▼ **Apply wax resist** When the painting has completely dried, rub a white candle randomly over the stonework areas.

6 ▶ **Apply a darker wash** Paint the line of roof tiles in burnt sienna. Leave to dry. Then mix Payne's grey and burnt sienna, and, using the No. 4 round brush, apply horizontal dabs of colour over the exposed stonework. The wash separates over the waxy areas, introducing a random effect.

7 ◀ **Paint the window grille** With washes of Payne's grey, ivory black and a Payne's grey/burnt sienna mix, start to paint the barred window. In the top half of the window, you are painting the dark shadows cast on the wall of the interior; in the lower half you are painting the bars themselves and the shadows that they cast.

8 ◀ **Apply more resist** Rub the candle randomly over the stonework to create another layer of resist. Mix a darker version of the Payne's grey/ burnt sienna wash from step 7 and apply dabs of colour with the No.4 round brush. Allow to dry, then apply another layer of wax resist, and a final layer of wash, using a dry brush.

Express yourself
Surface textures

To become more familiar with painting stonework and other building materials, find locations with a variety of hard surfaces and make rapid watercolour sketches that convey their qualities as simply as possible. Here the artist has used the white of the paper and washes of pink and yellow to suggest the even surface of painted stucco on the houses by the canal. The dressed stonework of the old bridge is deftly described with freely drawn lines and dappled washes of colour. Suggest the outlines of the stone blocks, without making the marks too mechanical or overworked.

9 ▲ **Remove the masking fluid** Paint the stained edge of the roof tiles and the shadow below the tiles in Payne's grey. Leave to dry. Mix Naples yellow and cobalt blue, and paint the foliage on the left. Make sure the support is dry, then lightly rub off the masking fluid.

10 ▲ **Add tone to the plaster** Use variations of the buff mix from step 3 to apply texture to the plaster, using a dry No. 8 round brush. Mix Payne's grey and lemon yellow, and dab on this grey-green colour under the eaves.

11 ▲ **Complete the foreground** Use Payne's grey for the hanging cables and creepers, burnt sienna for the window, and the buff mix from step 3 at the base of the building. Brush in the grass with a lemon yellow/Payne's grey mix, adding more Payne's grey to paint the road.

THE FINISHED PICTURE

A Masked edges
The complicated edges of the damaged stucco were defined with masking fluid, so the exposed brickwork could be worked on freely.

B Wax resist
Alternate layers of watercolour wash and wax resist applied with a candle gave the stonework a randomly mottled appearance.

C Linear detail
A buff mix skimmed over the surface of the NOT paper with a dry brush created a patchy, weathered effect on the stuccoed wall.

Leaping salmon

The flicker of silver as salmon leap up a cascade of water provides one of nature's most thrilling wildlife spectacles – and a great subject for a loose, lively watercolour.

Water tumbling down falls and churning over a boulder-strewn riverbed simply demands to be recorded in paint. But how do you capture the lightness and brightness of the broken water without making it look too solid or laboured? Watercolour, with its potential for spontaneous effects, is the ideal medium for such a dynamic and free-flowing subject.

Spattering techniques

Spattering, for instance, is easily done with watercolour. It creates a speckled or mottled surface ideal for depicting subjects such as foam, spray and turbulent water, which are too intricate to render in any other way. Soft-fibre brushes are the best for flicking colour.

Spattering with masking fluid was also used in this painting to preserve the white of the paper for light areas such as foam and spray. To avoid damaging the bristles, you should try flicking and dribbling the fluid from the handle of your brush (or use an old brush).

Masking fluid is available in two forms: colourless or tinted (yellow or grey). The advantage of using tinted fluid, as here, is that you can see exactly where the masked areas are.

Establishing the focus

Confidence is the key to success in this painting. Rather than working from light to dark in the usual watercolour way, the artist began by establishing the dark forms of the salmon. It is important that they are introduced early on as the composition pivots around their sinuous bodies. Use bold, assertive brush strokes – you do not want to have to rework or modify them. (If necessary, practise painting on scrap paper first.)

Continue working in this confident, uninhibited way throughout the painting. Use dilute paint and gestural strokes to capture the tumbling water. Vary the colour of your washes and let them blend spontaneously – remember water picks up reflected colour from its surroundings and from the sky above. In short, try to bring something of the drama of the subject to the way you paint it.

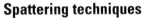

▼ Spattered paint, vigorous brush marks and bold contrasts of tone help to capture the drama of salmon leaping in foaming water.

YOU WILL NEED

Piece of 300gsm (140lb) NOT watercolour paper 44 x 56cm (17¼ x 22in)

B pencil

Masking fluid

11 watercolours: Prussian blue; cerulean blue; neutral tint; sepia; light red; cobalt blue; ultramarine; violet; raw umber; raw sienna; emerald green

Brushes: 13mm (½in) flat; No. 9 round

Mixing palette or dish

Jar of water

White chalk

FIRST STEPS

1 ▲ **Spatter masking fluid** Use a B pencil to plot the location of the leaping fish. Dip the handle of a brush in masking fluid and flick and dribble the fluid on to the surface of the paper. Build up an area of dense spattering on the left to balance the fish on the right, then apply spattered masking fluid to the foaming water below the fish.

2 ▲ **Block in the first fish** Mix Prussian blue and cerulean blue. Using a fairly dry 13mm (½in) flat brush, describe the back of the fish with a sweeping stroke. Drag the brush over the pitted surface of the paper so that the wash breaks up in places to create a slightly speckled effect. While the first wash is still wet, charge the same brush with a mix of neutral tint and sepia, and use this to describe the underside of the fish. Leave the stripe and eye area white, but allow the two washes to blend and fuse where they touch.

4 ▲ **Spatter around the tail** Paint the fish's tail with the neutral tint and light red, then drag the handle of the brush through the wet paint to suggest its ribbed pattern. Load the brush with a dark mix from your palette and lightly spatter across the spray around the tail.

3 ▲ **Work on the second fish** Using the same brush, paint the second fish. Use neutral tint for the upper body and light red for the belly of the fish. Add the fins in neutral tint and light red.

5 ▲ **Start to paint the water** Apply vigorous strokes of cobalt blue with the 13mm (½in) flat brush, then ultramarine with a touch of violet, followed by raw umber. Use gestural brush marks that trace the movement of the water. Allow the paint to flow together and puddle.

6 ▲ **Develop broken water** Start to apply colour over the heavily spattered area with broad strokes. Use washes of neutral tint, sepia, ultramarine, violet and Prussian blue, allowing the colours to mingle.

7 ◄ Add more colour to the water Still using the 13mm (½in) brush, apply a raw umber wash to the dark area in the lower left corner of the picture with vigorous brush marks. Work a pale wash of cobalt blue into the top left of the picture area.

DEVELOPING THE PICTURE

The painting is broadly established and this is a good time to stand back and see what else needs to be done. With a subject such as this, the reference photograph is a jumping-off point only – after a certain point the painting takes on a life of its own. The marks that you have made and the colours that you use will dictate your next moves.

8 ► Add warm colours Mix a wash of raw sienna, adding a touch of raw umber, and scumble this colour loosely over the lower part of the painting. This will warm the area of the painting, providing a contrast with the predominantly cool palette.

► A range of blues and browns was used for the wet-on-wet washes and spattering to create subtly shifting tones and splashes of colour in the turbulent water. The colours include (from top to bottom): cerulean blue; cobalt blue; ultramarine; violet; sepia.

9 ▲ Add textural marks Mix Prussian blue and raw umber and work this into the dark area on the left. Use gestural flicking marks that suggest the splashing water. Spatter the same mix across the painting.

10▼ **Spatter more colours** Wash emerald green across the lower right corner and spatter over it, creating texture with the brush handle (see Expert Advice, opposite). Add raw umber and apply loosely at top left. Spatter this mix and cerulean blue over the entire painting.

Express yourself

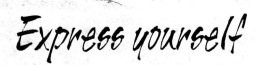

Fish studies

The streamlined bodies of fish form wonderful, sinuous shapes as they flash through the water or leap up the rapids. To familiarize yourself with their movements, it is a useful exercise to make pencil sketches of fish viewed from different angles. Notice the positions of the fins and the curves of the tails as they power the fish along.

These sketches will help you when making an initial drawing for a fish painting. In the step-by-step, the bodies of the salmon are implied with just a few sweeping brush strokes, so it is important that your underlying drawing is in proportion and accurately reflects the leaping motion.

11▲ **Remove the masking fluid** Make sure the painting is completely dry, then remove the masking fluid by rubbing it gently with your fingertips. As the mask is removed, the sparkling white paper is revealed as foam, spray and swirling water, making sense of the brushed and spattered colour.

A FEW STEPS FURTHER

With the masked areas revealed, the painting assumes its final appearance. The energy of the surging water has been effectively described and the composition is nicely balanced with the dark forms of the fish silhouetted against the foaming water. At this point you could consider emphasizing the tonal contrasts by adding highlights and touches of dark tone.

12▲ **Suggest the scales of the fish** Drag a piece of white chalk over the surface of the fish. The powdery chalk will be deposited on the raised surface of the paper, suggesting silvery scales.

13 ▼ **Contrast tones** Scumble chalk across the darker areas of water. Mix a wash of neutral tint and Prussian blue and, using a No. 9 round brush, spatter on this dark tone.

EXPERT ADVICE
Drawing out paint

To create linear texture in spattered areas, draw out the wet paint into squiggly strands and tendrils of colour with the tip of the brush handle. Here, raw sienna and raw umber provide texture over an emerald green wash.

THE FINISHED PICTURE

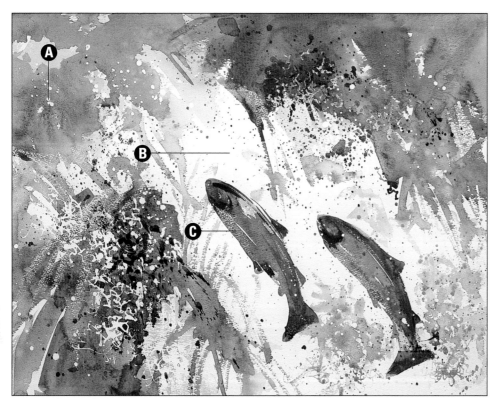

A Masked spatters
The patterns created by masking fluid spattered on to the support at the start read as foam and spray when the mask is removed.

B White paper
Extensive areas of unpainted white paper stand for the sheets of white water cascading down the waterfall.

C Scumbled chalk
Chalk scumbled over the pitted surface of the paper adds a bright, sparkling effect and lends texture to the solid washes.

Japanese bridge

A bold, uncluttered composition, a restrained palette of cool blues and greens, and a vivid splash of red produce a lyrical and memorable image.

The delicate and transparent washes of watercolour are ideal for this beautiful misty landscape. By building up layers of colour, you can capture the depth of the water and the deep, cool greens of the leafy foliage. What's more, you can use wet-on-wet techniques to create the hazy appearance of the mist-shrouded hills and wet-on-dry techniques to add crisp details, such as the structure of the bridge and the thin outer branches of the trees.

Considered composition

Before you actually begin working on any painting, make sure you consider the compositional possibilities. In this project, the eye is drawn to the area of light water in the foreground, where the sky is reflected in the lake's surface, then on to the even paler area under the bridge and hence to the bridge itself. The arcing form of the bridge frames the lower part of the painting, as do the dark blocks of foliage on the left and right. In the distance, the misty peaks allow air into the composition and prevent it from becoming claustrophobic. Note also that, as there is no foreground detail, the whole composition seems flattened just like a Japanese print.

When considering the composition, take time to look for similarities and differences. In this picture, the curved lines of the banks in the foreground are echoed by the curved tops of the mountains in the distance – and indeed by the arc of the bridge. These gentle curves are perfectly offset by the spiky edge of the tree on the left.

Complementary colours

As should always be the case, the use of colour in the picture is equally well thought out. The hot, insistent red of the bridge is set off by the cool, complementary greens of the foliage and the paler hills in the background. Note how the hills have a pinkish tinge, while the foreground is painted in much cooler blues and greens.

▶ **Subtle changes of colour and tone create a mood of peace and tranquillity in this watercolour painting of a classic Japanese view.**

Piece of 300gsm (140lb) NOT watercolour paper 56 x 46cm (22 x 18in)

HB pencil

10 watercolours: ultramarine; Prussian blue; alizarin crimson; viridian; sap green; raw umber; cadmium red; Van Dyke brown; ivory black; yellow ochre

Brushes: 25mm (1in) hake; Nos. 12 and 4 rounds

Permanent white gouache

Mixing palette or dish

FIRST STEPS

1 ▼ Make the underdrawing Using an HB pencil, sketch in the main outlines of the composition. Work lightly, so that the pencil lines do not dominate the final image, and make any necessary adjustments to the drawing and composition at this stage.

2 ◄ Block in the sky Mix a pale wash of ultramarine and Prussian blue, and, using the broad 25mm (1in) hake brush, apply the wash to the sky. Take the colour along the edge of the hills.

3 ► Paint the hills The background hills overlap like the flats in a theatre set. The interlocking shapes vary in colour and tone, depending on how far away they are, with those in the background looking paler than those nearer the foreground. Mix a watery wash of ultramarine, alizarin crimson and Prussian blue, and, using a No. 12 round brush, paint the hills in the background.

▶ **Prussian blue, ultramarine and alizarin crimson give a range of pale blues and lilacs for the hills in the distance.**

Express yourself
Pastel impression

Soft pastel is a great medium for creating misty effects. Use mauves and purples for the hills and river, applying the pastel lightly and smudging it back for distant features. Sharply drawn linear details bring the foliage forwards.

4 ▲ **Intensify the hills** Add more alizarin crimson to the wash and, working wet-on-wet, intensify the hills in the centre, so that they come forward in the scene. Add more ultramarine and Prussian blue to create a cooler mix for the hills on the right. Also, indicate the trees on the hills (see Expert Advice, below).

EXPERT ADVICE
Silhouetted trees

The treetops on the distant hills, seen through the mist, form hazy, spire-like silhouettes against the sky. Use the tip of the No. 12 round brush to mark these in wet-on-wet, so that they merge into the overall wash covering the hills.

5 ◀ **Suggest the trees** Add more Prussian blue to the cool blue mix from step 4. Still using the No. 12 round brush, stroke on this colour to represent the area of trees cladding the lower slopes of the hills on the left. Vary the texture with a stronger version of the same mix.

DEVELOPING THE PICTURE

Now move to the area below the bridge to start work on the cool blue water of the river, which relates in colour and tone to the sky and hills. Then progress to the stronger tones of the trees and foliage that frame the composition at the sides, and the painting will really start to come alive.

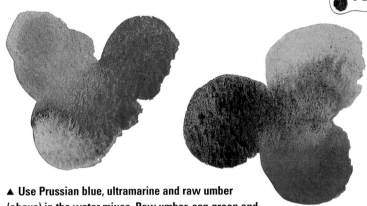

▲ **Use Prussian blue, ultramarine and raw umber (above) in the water mixes. Raw umber, sap green and Prussian blue (right) produce dark foliage shades.**

6 ▼ Add more trees Use viridian, sap green and ultramarine to create a grey-green for the trees fringing the river beyond the bridge. Use the brush tip to create the treetops. Add sap green and raw umber to the mix from step 3 and dilute with more water. Wash this pale tone over the river. Use ultramarine and Prussian blue for the darker water at the edges of the river.

7 ▼ Develop wooded areas Mix a dark green from sap green, Prussian blue and raw umber, and, using the No. 12 round brush and gestural marks, start to build up shadows within the clump of trees on the left.

8 ▼ Add more foliage Continuing with the No. 12 round, use a wash of ultramarine and sap green for the mass of bright green foliage on the left.

9 ▲ Paint more trees Using the same dark wash as in step 7, dab on the shadows within the trees on the right. Then return to the light green wash from step 8 and paint in the brighter foliage where the trees catch the light.

10 ▼ **Add the bridge** The bridge is the key to the whole composition. Mix cadmium red and alizarin crimson, and start to paint the bridge, using a No. 4 round brush. Work carefully, checking the reference photograph for the lattice-work pattern.

11 ▶ **Add shadows** Mix a dark brown from Van Dyke brown and ivory black. Returning to the No. 12 round brush, paint the shadows on the pillars that support the bridge. Then block in the curve of dark tone that forms the base of the bridge.

12 ◀ **Paint between the lattice** When the dark shadows are dry, use a paler version of the dark brown mix for the lighter areas of the bridge supports and for the rocks edging the water. Paint the landscape seen between the lattice-work with the No. 4 brush and a mix of sap green and ultramarine.

13 ▶ **Develop the foreground water**
Make a mix of Prussian blue and ultramarine, and, changing back to the No. 12 brush, apply the shadows along the water's edge and in the foreground. Use brushy horizontal marks to show the ripples on the surface of the water.

14 ▲ **Add shadows to the foliage** Use a mix of sap green, ultramarine and raw umber, and the tip of the No. 12 brush, to paint the shadows within the clumps of foliage on the right. These dark tones in the foliage help to describe the layering of branches and enhance the sense of depth within the tree canopy.

15 ▲ **Darken the water** Use a dark mix of Prussian blue, ultramarine and raw umber to add tone and depth to the edges of the water. Touch in the finials on the bridge posts and add texture to the base with a black/Van Dyke brown mix.

A FEW STEPS FURTHER

The painting is now fully resolved. All the elements are in place, and the spatial progression from front to back works well. You could add a few details, such as the fine branches on the tree and white highlights for the brass embellishments on the bridge. Be careful not to overwork the image, however, or you will lose the freshness of the watercolour.

16 ▲ **Add brass highlights** Mix yellow ochre with white gouache. Using the No. 4 round, apply this pale opaque mix to the finials and to the decorations on top of each upright.

17 ▲ **Add the branches** Mix Van Dyke brown and ultramarine, and use the tip of the No. 4 round to draw in the thin branches visible through the outer edges of the tree canopy. Work out towards the ends of the branches to achieve strokes that taper at the tip.

THE FINISHED PICTURE

A Layered greens
Layers of transparent green washes capture the depth, density and delicacy of the foliage bordering the river.

B Body colour
Opaque body colour mixed from white gouache and yellow ochre makes the metalwork sparkle.

C Paper highlights
Light catching the water is suggested by allowing the white paper to shimmer through a pale wash.

Scottish landscapes

You will need just four simple shades of watercolour to create these atmospheric studies of the beautiful Scottish countryside.

For the watercolour artist, a limited palette can be a great advantage, especially if you are painting outdoors and want to capture the scene quickly. The two landscapes on the following pages were painted using the same four colours: cadmium red, gamboge, ultramarine and Davy's grey. By varying the proportions of these four basic tints in each mixture, you can create an almost limitless range of colours and tones.

For example, the misty Scottish loch above contains lots of hazy blues and purples. These were mixed mainly from cadmium red, ultramarine and Davy's grey, but with a few streaks of gamboge to indicate sunlight.

The moorland landscape, by contrast, is dominated by the vast expanse of grass in the foreground. For this painting the artist worked mainly in ultramarine and gamboge, with occasional touches of grey and red.

Granulation and brushwork

Both landscapes were painted quickly, but each wash of colour was allowed to dry naturally before the next layer of colour was applied. The extra drying time allowed the pigment particles to disperse on the surface of the paper, creating the

▲ Cool purples predominate in this painting of a Scottish loch with a background of mountains and brooding clouds.

beautiful granular textures that can be seen in the finished paintings. (If you use a hair-dryer to speed up the process, you might diminish this effect.)

Brushwork in both landscapes is lively and bold. Decorator's brushes and a large wash brush were used to establish broad sweeps of sky, water and grassy foreground. In addition, the artist deliberately worked with an old, worn-out brush to create sharp, spiky shapes.

PROJECT 1

SCOTTISH LOCH

In the first project, the four basic watercolours are used in loose washes to convey the damp, misty atmosphere of a lake and mountains on a cloudy day. Wet-on-wet effects create beautiful blends of colour.

1 ▲ **Wash in the sky** Define your picture area with masking tape, then use a propelling pencil to lightly mark in the water's edge and the skyline. Mix a thin, purplish wash of ultramarine with a little cadmium red and Davy's grey, and loosely block in the sky, using a 25mm (1in) soft flat brush. Paint pure gamboge along the skyline, allowing this to run into the wet sky.

▲ **Cadmium red, ultramarine and gamboge correspond to the three primary colours. From these three colours plus Davy's grey, you can mix the range of violet-based colours that predominate in this scene.**

2 ◄ **Apply a wash to the water** Dip a 38mm (1½in) decorator's brush into the purple wash, then pick up a little pure gamboge on the tips of the bristles. Apply the colours horizontally along the water's edge, allowing the yellow and purple to mix on the paper. Drag the wet colours downwards, using vertical brush strokes. Allow the paint to dry.

EXPERT ADVICE
Granulation effects

Whenever you can, allow the watercolour paint to dry naturally. In this way, the pigment particles will disperse unevenly and create beautiful granulated effects, seen here in the sky.

3 ▲ Add the background Paint the hills with mixes of ultramarine, cadmium red and added touches of gamboge, making some of the mixes quite dilute. Use an old, misshapen brush to achieve spiky, irregular brush strokes.

Express yourself
Moody effects in the landscape

Watercolour lends itself perfectly to rendering landscapes with moody, cloud-strewn skies over hills and lakes, as no other medium captures quite so well the muted colours and indistinct shapes created by a misty atmosphere. In this variation of the Scottish loch scene, wet-on-wet effects are used for the clouds hanging over the mountaintops. Notice how the wash used for the low cloud on the right has formed a crinkled 'cauliflower' edge where the pigment has spread and dried.

4 ▼ **Suggest the shore** Block in the central hill with a dilute wash of ultramarine and cadmium red. Then add Davy's grey to this mix to get a stronger colour and use the No. 6 round brush to define the shore with short, horizontal strokes.

5 ▲ **Develop the water** Add a splash of cadmium red at the centre of the shoreline. Then change to a 19mm (¾in) decorator's brush and, working in broad, horizontal strokes, strengthen the water with a wash of ultramarine and Davy's grey. Leave streaks of underpainting showing through between the brush strokes.

6 ▼ **Add reflections** Still using the 19mm (¾in) decorator's brush, drag the wet colour downwards in the foreground to indicate the reflections on the water.

7 ▲ **Put in some tree details** Use the No. 6 round brush and ultramarine to add details of clumps of trees along the shoreline on the right-hand side. Allow the painting to dry, then remove the masking tape.

THE FINISHED PICTURE

A Directional strokes
The sky is blocked in loosely, taking the brush in different directions to create an impression of moving clouds.

B Spiky background
Some of the trees and shrubs seen in silhouette on the distant shore are painted with irregular strokes, using an old, worn brush.

C Vertical reflections
Wet colour is dragged downwards with a broad brush to suggest reflections on the surface of the water.

PROJECT 2

RAILWAY BRIDGE

In this watercolour project, the barren moorland is interrupted only by shrubs and a railway bridge in the middle distance. As in the first project, mountains shrouded by clouds form a dramatic backdrop.

1 ▼ Apply an overall wash Define your picture area with masking tape, then mix a thin grey wash from gamboge and Davy's grey. Using a 38mm (1½in) decorator's brush and working in loose strokes, cover the entire picture area. Add a little more grey as you work down the

▼ Mixing gamboge and ultramarine with a dash of red produces the basic green shade used in the landscape.

2 ▼ Draw the subject Allow the grey wash to dry, then use a propelling pencil to draw the outline of the hills and to indicate the position of the bridge.

3 ▼ Develop the sky Using a 25mm (1in) decorator's brush, block in the hills with a mix of ultramarine and Davy's grey. Add a little gamboge to the mix and use this to darken the sky. Work in crisscross strokes and leave areas of the paler underpainting showing through.

▼ These swatches show some of the soft, subtle landscape tints that you can create from the four colours used in the two projects. The labels indicate the colour or colours that predominate in each mix.

| Gamboge/ cadmium red | Cadmium red | Ultramarine/ Davy's grey | Ultramarine | Ultramarine/ gamboge | Gamboge |

4 ▶ Block in the foreground Mix a strong yellow-green wash from gamboge and ultramarine with a touch of cadmium red. Using a 25mm (1in) soft flat brush, apply this in broad horizontal strokes to block in the foreground grass – leave the occasional streak of underpainting showing through between the brush strokes. Add one or two streaks of neat gamboge and allow this to merge with the wet green. Leave the painting to dry.

5 ▼ Use a dry brush Change to a No. 6 round brush to suggest the background shrubs and bridge. Use the brush dry, dipping the bristle tips into green and purple mixtures of ultramarine, gamboge and Davy's grey, and applying the colour in short strokes for a spiky effect.

6 ▲ Add a dab of warm colour Finally, add a dab of pure cadmium red to the background. The bright colour sings out against the muted shades of the rest of the painting.

THE FINISHED PICTURE

A Pure sunlight
Streaks of gamboge painted wet-on-wet in the foreground create an effective impression of sunlight on grass.

B Focal point
A small dab of warm red was the artist's inventive addition to the scene – it becomes a focal point and draws the eye into the picture.

C Dry-brush technique
The bridge is suggested with strokes of dark tone applied with a dry brush.

Boat on a beach

Using masking fluid with watercolour will help you to capture the wonderful array of textures in this seaside scene.

A relatively simple subject can be lifted by paying attention to details and textures. In this project the knobbly textures of the shingle beach, together with its subtle variations of colour and tone, complement the clean, uncluttered lines of the boat.

Creating a shingle effect

The problem of rendering the complex appearance of the myriad pebbles on the beach can be solved quickly and easily by using masking fluid. When this milky liquid is applied to a support, it dries to a film that protects the underlying surface from subsequent paint applications. Usually used directly on white paper to create pure white areas, it can also be spattered over washes to reserve a particular colour or tone.

The shingle effect here is created by spattering masking fluid on to the previously toned support, with the small droplets creating a pebble-like pattern. A layer of wash slightly darker than the ground colour is then applied and allowed to dry. Several more layers of masking fluid are spattered over the beach area, alternated with washes of watercolour that gradually become darker in tone. When all the layers of masking fluid are finally removed, the pebble-shaped areas beneath the droplets are revealed.

Net texture

The same approach is used to render the mesh-like pattern of the heap of fishing nets in the foreground. Here the masking fluid is applied with a dip pen over a mid-toned blue in a pattern of fine crisscross lines. A darker wash is then brushed on so that the strands of the net will stand out light against dark when the mask is removed. A second application of masking fluid and wash adds depth to the heap of netting.

▶ **The beach is cleverly depicted by alternating spattered masking fluid with watercolour washes.**

Piece of 300gsm (140lb) NOT watercolour paper 27 x 34cm (10½ x 13½in)

2B pencil

Paint shaper

Masking fluid

Toothbrush

Scrap paper

14 watercolours: cobalt blue; alizarin crimson; yellow ochre; Winsor blue; raw umber; burnt sienna; cadmium lemon; ultramarine; indigo; Payne's grey; Winsor green; light red; cadmium orange; cadmium red

Brushes: Nos. 8 and 3 rounds

Dip pen

FIRST STEPS

1 ▲ **Sketch the scene** Use a 2B pencil to outline the boat and the heaped fishing nets, then mark in the flags and the planks that lead the eye into the scene. Now, using a paint shaper, apply masking fluid around the edge of the boat, and over the planks, flags and nets. Dot masking fluid on to the foreground of the beach, too, to reserve the shapes of the larger pebbles.

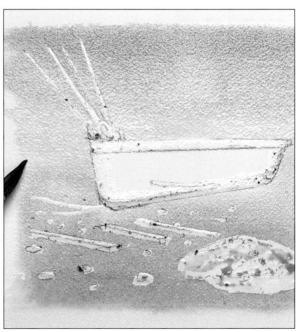

2 ▲ **Lay in the sky and beach** Use a No. 8 round brush to wet the paper and then flood in a mix of cobalt blue with a touch of alizarin crimson, starting at the top of the paper. Add more water to the mix as you bring the wash down the paper to the horizon line, in order to create a gradated wash. Mix a wash of yellow ochre and flood this on to the beach. Leave to dry.

3 ▶ Darken the horizon Wet the horizon with a No. 3 round brush. Mix a wash of Winsor blue and apply this along the horizon line so that it floods into the wet area to give a softly diffused edge. Apply a wash of raw umber below the Winsor blue and leave to dry.

4 ▼ Spatter on masking fluid Load an old toothbrush with masking fluid, then tap the brush against your hand to deposit droplets of masking fluid over the beach area. Leave to dry.

5 ▲ Apply a wash over the beach Mix burnt sienna and cadmium lemon, and, using the No. 8 round brush, wash this over the foreground. Leave to dry.

6 ▲ Apply more spatter and wash Spatter another layer of masking fluid over the beach, as in step 4. Mix a darker tone of the burnt sienna and cadmium lemon wash, and apply over the beach.

Express yourself

Into the blue

In this study, the focus is on the bright blue fishing boat rather than the beach. The artist has again opted for watercolour, but this time he has relied on a simple combination of wet-on-wet and dry-brush techniques. The boat itself is painted in strong tones of ultramarine, and with its vivid red trim it really stands out from the beach. The bold, white lettering, created by leaving the paper untouched, gives it even greater emphasis. The beach on the other hand is very loosely worked in pale tones of grey and raw umber. A little black has been flooded on to the wet beach to stand for the shadows under the boat.

To control the size of the spattered droplets, make sure you don't overload the toothbrush with masking fluid. If the brush is too heavily loaded, the masking fluid will form droplets that are too large. Remove surplus fluid by tapping the brush over scrap paper.

7 ▲ Apply more spattering Once the previous wash has dried, apply another layer of spattered masking fluid to the beach. Leave to dry.

8 ▲ Apply darker washes Mix burnt sienna with ultramarine and wash over the beach. Allow to dry, then apply another layer of spattered masking fluid, followed by a further wash of the same mix. When that is dry, apply more spattered masking fluid. Once this is dry, apply the same mix darkened with a touch of indigo. Leave to dry.

9 ▲ Spatter paint Mask off the areas above and below the beach with scrap paper. Load the No. 8 brush with a wash of Payne's grey and spatter dark droplets over the beach, moving the brush over the surface to get even coverage. Leave to dry.

DEVELOPING THE PICTURE

Now that the shingle – the most complex element of the picture – has been fully resolved, remove the masking fluid and move on to tackle the boat and the debris lying on the beach.

10 ▶ Remove the masking fluid When the support is thoroughly dry, remove the masking fluid from the beach by rubbing gently with the tips of your fingers. Notice how the layers of spattered masking fluid have reserved different layers of wash to give a wide range of pebble shades. Remove the masking fluid from the boat, the pile of nets and the planks to reveal crisp, white shapes.

11 ◄ **Work up the foreground** Mix Winsor blue, Winsor green and Payne's grey, then paint the nets with the No. 3 round. Load the brush with a mix of ultramarine and indigo and apply shadows to the underside of some of the larger stones. Apply a wash of burnt sienna and Winsor blue over the planks.

12 ▲ **Paint the boat** Apply burnt sienna with a touch of indigo along the top edge of the boat, leaving the highlight as unpainted white paper. Wet the highlit area below the brown band with clean water, then paint the hull around the wet area with cobalt blue – the colour will flow in at the edges to create a gradated tone.

13 ▲ **Add details to the boat** Apply a line of light red along the keel, then paint an indigo shadow, letting the colours blend wet-on-wet. Use the tip of the brush and a thin wash of burnt sienna to paint the flag poles. To capture movement in the flags, first paint the flag tips with clean water. Then apply indigo to the flags, allowing the colour to bleed softly into the fluttering tips.

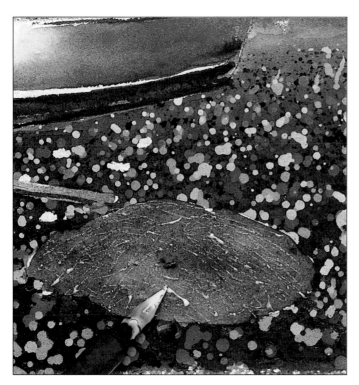

16 ▲ **Remove the masking fluid** When the final wash is completely dry, lightly rub over the net area to remove the masking fluid and reveal a mesh of paler lines.

14 ▲ **Apply masking fluid to the pile of nets** Paint shadows on the sides of the planks with a mix of Payne's grey and raw umber. Now load a dip pen with masking fluid and draw a fine mesh of lines over the nets – the firm, pointed nib gives you considerable control. Leave to dry.

A FEW STEPS FURTHER

The painting is fully established, with the pebbles and boat convincingly rendered. Only a few details are needed to complete the image: some lines to show the timber construction of the boat and the groyne in the distance, and a couple of red flags to provide a touch of visual excitement.

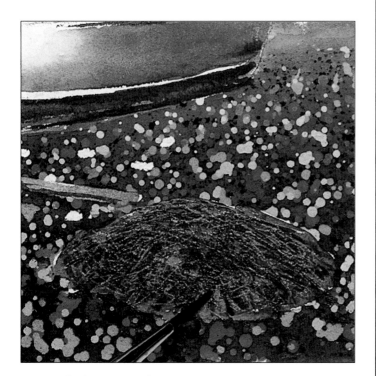

15 ▲ **Apply a wash to the nets** Mix Winsor blue with indigo and, using the No. 3 round brush, apply a wash of colour over the heap of nets. Leave to dry. Use the dip pen and masking fluid to apply a further mesh of lines over the netting. Leave to dry, then apply another layer of Winsor blue/indigo wash. Leave to dry.

17 ▲ **Add planks** Use the tip of the No. 3 round brush and Payne's grey to indicate the overlapping planks on the boat's hull. Indicate the shadows under the boat and the planks on which it is resting.

18 ▶ Add some detail around the stern
Use the burnt sienna/ indigo mix from step 12 to fill in the white strip along the side of the boat. With the tip of the No. 3 round brush and Payne's grey, add fine details and shadows around the stern of the boat. Define the top edge of the boat with a narrow line of Payne's grey to crisp up the outline.

19 ▲ Add red flags Using Payne's grey, put in patchy shadows at the base of the flag poles and flick in the groyne in the distance. Mix cadmium orange and cadmium red to paint the red flags, as described in step 13.

THE FINISHED PICTURE

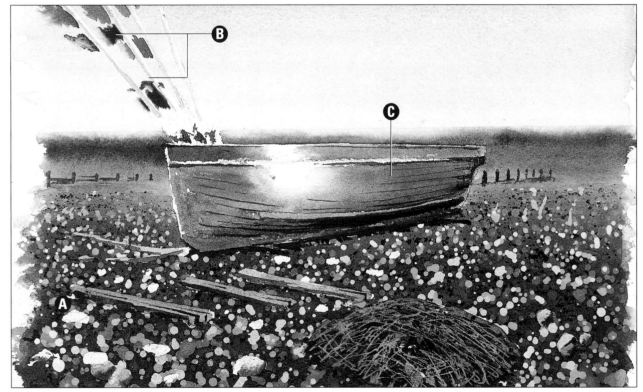

A Graded stones
Lumps of white chalk (paper reserved with masking fluid) lead the eye around the foreground. They are carefully graded in size to help the illusion of recession in the scene.

B Eye-catching red
The bright, insistent colour of the two red flags contrasts with the predominant blues and browns, and provides an eye-catching focus that draws the viewer into the picture.

C Sense of scale
The simply rendered groyne gives a sense of depth, allowing the eye to read the spatial recession, from the boat and shingle in the foreground to the sea in the distance.

Poppies in a landscape

If your ideal landscape doesn't exist, why not create it from various sources and with a little artistic licence?

This glorious landscape with its jubilant poppies bordering a field of golden corn doesn't exist in reality. The painting is a fabrication – a work in which a still-life set-up and a landscape photograph, plus a dose of imagination, come together to create a totally plausible composition.

The photo of a luxuriant green field, a farmhouse and an ancient stone wall bordering the field (top right) formed the basis of the work, although it is considerably altered, both in content and in colour. Green fields became yellow cornfields; greyish hills became purple; stone walls vanished from view.

The poppies, which give a burst of red in the foreground, were based on a bunch of bought poppies (right). These provided an ideal visual reference.

▼ The poppies and grasses that dominate the foreground contrast in scale with the distant cottage, setting up a strong feeling of recession in the scene.

FIRST STEPS

1 ▼ **Plan the composition** Using a brown water-soluble pencil (it will wash out when you paint over it), sketch the distant hills and house. Place the poppies in the foreground, making them very large to give the sense of a receding landscape.

YOU WILL NEED

Piece of 300gsm (140lb) watercolour paper 36 x 46cm (14 x 18in)

Brown water-soluble coloured pencil

9 watercolours: cerulean blue; ultramarine; alizarin crimson; cadmium red; cadmium yellow pale; Winsor green; lemon

yellow; yellow ochre; burnt sienna

Brushes: Nos. 16 and 8 rounds; No. 2 rigger

Mixing palette or dish

Jar of water

Stiff card

Old toothbrush

2 ▼ **Start with the sky** Using a No. 16 round brush, wet the sky area, then go over it with sweeps of cerulean blue, followed by ultramarine. Use loose, curved brush strokes rather than broad, horizontal strokes.

3 ▲ **Mix a purple** Combine alizarin crimson with ultramarine to make a purple, and use this both within the sky and on the furthest hill. Although the hill appears blue-grey in the photo, you can adapt the colours if you wish. To create some warmer accents, wash areas of cadmium red into the landscape.

▼ **To prevent the red and purple mixes (left) from accidentally running into the blues and greens (below), the artist used two palettes.**

4 ◄ **Paint with water** Move forward in the scene, painting the distant fields with mixes of cerulean blue, cadmium yellow pale and Winsor green. To create a hazy effect, dip the brush in clean water and use it to slice across the sky and hills, lifting and blending the colours as you do so.

5 ▼ **Establish the cornfield** Transform the grassy field of the photograph into a cornfield by washing lemon yellow over the foreground area. Use the No. 16 round brush for this, taking care to avoid the poppies.

DEVELOPING THE PICTURE

With the broad areas of the landscape blocked in, turn your attention to the details in the scene – the house, the clumps of trees and the poppies in the foreground.

6 ▲ **Paint the farmhouse** Switch to a No. 2 rigger and cadmium red to outline the farmhouse and paint the windows. Now, with a No. 8 round brush, paint the roof and side of the house. Brush clean water on to the side wall, and draw some of the colour down from the roof to create a pale tone.

7 ▼ **Put in the trees** A line of trees spans the middle distance. Paint these with mixes of Winsor green and yellow ochre, varying the proportions of the colours to create visual interest.

8 ▶ **Fill in the poppies** With the No. 2 rigger, define the doorway of the house, the roof and the side wall in Winsor green. Then, with the No. 8 round brush, start painting the poppies. Use varying strengths of cadmium red for the flower-heads, with occasional touches of lemon yellow.

EXPERT ADVICE
Printing techniques

Printing with the edge of a card strip is a useful way to make thin lines for stems. Don't dip the card into the paint, as it will become saturated and messy. Instead, use a brush to paint colour on to the edge of the card.

Express yourself
Change of format

Within a landscape, real or imaginary, there are often various ways of cropping into the scene to produce new and equally interesting compositions. Here, the artist has focused more closely on the farmhouse in the middle distance by cropping off the sides of the original composition, creating an unusually tall and narrow format. The verticals of the poppies and grasses in the foreground fill the paper from top to bottom, cutting across the view and bringing the viewer even closer into the scene than in the conventional landscape format. The sense of distance created by contrasting warm and cool colours is, however, just as strong.

9 ▼ **Print with card** Using the edge of a strip of stiff card (see Expert Advice, opposite), print narrow lines to stand for the dried grasses – yellow ochre on the left, burnt sienna on the right. Bend another card strip to form a V-shape and print the ears of corn, beginning at the top of each stem. Again, use yellow ochre on some of the stems and burnt sienna on others.

10 ▲ **Print the fence** Using the No. 2 rigger, strengthen the cadmium red roof of the house and add details to the windows, chimney and wall with burnt sienna and ultramarine. Then, changing to the No. 8 round, block in the foreground fence-posts with burnt sienna. Print Winsor green outlines with a card strip.

11 ▼ **Provide some dark accents** Use the No. 2 rigger and Winsor green to dot in the dark centres on the poppies. Mix ultramarine and burnt sienna to define the background hills.

12 ▲ **Build up the foreground** With the No. 2 rigger and a mix of alizarin crimson and ultramarine, define the brow of the hill in the centre by dotting dark accents along the ridge. To create visual interest in the foreground, print more hedgerow grasses, as in step 9. Use Winsor green for some and a dark mix of ultramarine and burnt sienna for others.

A FEW STEPS FURTHER

The landscape has a strong sense of recession, with the warm reds of the poppies throwing the mauves of the hills into distant relief. Complete the painting by adding a little more detail with the rigger and some spattering.

13 ▶ **Suggest some distant trees**
Return to the No. 2 rigger to add a clump of mauve-coloured trees at the top of the hill in the centre – use a dilute mix of alizarin crimson and ultramarine for this.

14 ▲ **Spatter texture** Load the bristles of an old toothbrush with burnt sienna. Draw the brush over some stiff card to spatter droplets of paint across the foreground and up into the sky.

THE FINISHED PICTURE

A Visual reference
The device of showing just the top of the fence in the foreground makes us feel that we are actually at the scene – spectators within a real landscape.

B Central landmark
The inclusion of the farmhouse in the middle distance, a recognizable landmark dwarfed by the poppies and grasses, reinforces the vast scale of the countryside.

C Sense of space
The cool hues of the hills on the horizon create a powerful sense of recession, particularly when contrasted with the warm colours in the foreground.

Picture postcards

Blank postcards made of watercolour paper are a great addition to a holiday painting kit – use them to send a unique record of your travels to your friends.

There is a long tradition of artists sending personalized decorated correspondence. Artists such as Marcel Duchamp (1887–1968) and Kurt Schwitters (1887–1948), for example, created individual picture postcards which they sent to friends and relatives. Why not follow in their footsteps and create your own watercolour postcards to send to your friends and relatives.

Holiday postcards

A holiday away from home is a good time to try painting your own postcards, as you'll have plenty of inspiring material to work from. The challenge is to produce an image that works on a small scale – the postcards often measure about 10.5 x 15cm (4 x 6in). The secret lies in the composition – if you underpin the painting with a good, simple line drawing, you will produce an image that engages the viewer.

Working methods

To help you find a suitable composition, half-close your eyes and look at how lights and darks are distributed across the subject. See, too, if you can find interesting divisions or repeated shapes in the scene. Some thumbnail sketches will help you explore the possibilities.

▲ **A combination of pencil, oil pastel and watercolour on postcard-sized watercolour paper gives impressive results quickly.**

When working on location, you'll need a portable kit. The combination of pencil, watercolour and oil pastel used for the two step-by-steps shown on the following pages is simple but effective.

The pencil is used to make fluent, calligraphic marks that contribute to the final image, rather than just plotting where the washes should go. Watercolour is a flexible medium that can be used for broad washes of transparent colour or for quite controlled detail. A small box of pan watercolours is an ideal option for the travelling artist, as it is light and the colours can be accessed directly. Tube colours are more cumbersome – using them involves deciding which colours you will need, fiddling about with lids and then squeezing out blobs of paint (some of which you may choose not to use after all).

Sticks of oil pastel are portable and produce solid patches of vibrant colour as well as line. These solid areas contrast with the transparency of the watercolour. Also, because oil and watercolour are incompatible, the oil pastel is unaffected by subsequent washes.

Because of its waxy quality, white oil pastel can be used as a form of resist – you can put it down on any areas of your painting that should read as white. You can then apply watercolour washes quite freely over the top. This method was used to retain the white windows on the building in the scene below. White oil pastel is more convenient than masking fluid, so is a useful addition to your travel kit.

PROJECT 1

PLAZA MAYOR, MADRID

A café table gives you a ringside seat from which to watch the world go by and discreetly make a record of the scene. Give the image structure by simplifying the architecture and emphasizing colours and shapes in the foreground.

1 ▶ Make a drawing Using a 3B pencil, plot the key verticals and horizontals, then add the chairs and tables in the foreground to give a sense of scale and depth. Work rapidly with fluent lines that give the drawing a sense of immediacy. Indicate the shadows within the arcade around the square.

YOU WILL NEED

Watercolour paper postcard 10.5 x 15cm (4 x 6in)	alizarin crimson; cadmium yellow; cadmium red
3B pencil	4 oil pastels: white; burnt orange; scarlet; crimson
8 watercolours: cerulean blue; cobalt blue; phthalo blue; ivory black; yellow ochre;	Brushes: Nos. 12 and 3 rounds

2 ▲ Lay in the sky Mix a pale wash of cerulean blue and cobalt blue and apply to the sky with a No. 12 round brush. Use phthalo blue for the table on the left and add a little ivory black for the table on the right. Describe the curving chair backs with the tip of a No. 3 brush.

3 ▲ Paint the buildings Using the No. 12 brush, mix yellow ochre, cobalt blue and alizarin crimson for the pale grey of the roofs, pavement and arcade. By adjusting the proportions of each colour, you can create subtle shifts in tone.

4 ▶ Apply oil pastel
Use a white oil pastel as a resist for the windows on the buildings – you can then wash over the façade without any fiddly brushwork. Dab colourful touches of burnt orange, scarlet and crimson oil pastel on to the parasols and the tables.

▲ The shades of maroon and brown used for the parasols are mixed from cadmium yellow, cadmium red, alizarin crimson and phthalo blue.

5 ▼ Paint the parasols For the orange parasols, mix cadmium yellow and cadmium red watercolour; apply with the No. 3 round. For the undersides and darker parasols, make various mixes of phthalo blue, alizarin crimson, cadmium red and cadmium yellow. Use a dilute mix for the building's façade. Mix phthalo blue and black to make a grey for the shadowy arcade.

6 ▲ Add details Use the grey mix for the lamppost. Combine phthalo blue with alizarin crimson, and wash over the shadow on the façade. Use the same colour and the reddish mixes from step 5 for linear details on the chair backs and umbrella poles.

THE FINISHED PICTURE

A White pastel resist
To avoid fiddly brushwork on the façade of the building, white oil pastel was worked over the windows in order to resist the watercolour wash.

B Lively pencil lines
A lively, fluent pencil line holds the image together and complements the loose painting style.

C Bright oil pastel
Emphatic touches of brightly coloured oil pastel add emphasis to the foreground, and encourage the viewer's eyes to dance across the foreground.

PROJECT 2

CHATEAU DE CHENONCEAUX, LOIRE

The turrets of the French château of Chenonceaux looming over the surrounding waters make a romantic subject that cries out to be painted. The soaring verticals of the towers pierce the broad triangle of the sky, while the dark water below provides visual stability.

YOU WILL NEED

Watercolour paper postcard
15 x 10.5cm (6 x 4in)

3B pencil

6 oil pastels: yellow ochre;
burnt sienna; black; blue;
grey; green

6 watercolours: yellow ochre;
alizarin crimson; raw umber;
cobalt blue; phthalo blue;
cerulean blue

Brushes: Nos. 12 and
3 rounds

1 ▶ Make a drawing
Using a 3B pencil, make a drawing of the château. Start with the line of the water's edge and some other key perspective lines such as decorative bands along the façade. Where these curve around the towers, they help to describe their cylindrical forms. All these perspective lines should meet at a single vanishing point which, in this case, is beyond the picture area. Plot the verticals of the towers and check proportions and angles with your pencil at arm's length.

2 ▶ Add oil pastel Using yellow ochre, burnt sienna and black oil pastels, touch in small areas of colour on the façade of the building, echoed by reflections in the surface of the water. With blue and grey oil pastels, add the cool shadows on the slate-covered roofs.

▲ Mixes of yellow ochre, alizarin crimson, cobalt blue and raw umber provide browns and greys for the château walls and their reflections.

3 ▸ Apply a wash Mix a wash of yellow ochre watercolour with a touch of alizarin crimson. Using a No. 12 round brush, loosely apply this ochre wash over the façade of the building to suggest the weathered character of the masonry. The tiny touches of opaque oil pastel applied in step 2 resist the watercolour, creating areas of lively, broken colour.

Express yourself
People in the picture

Holidays are as much about people as places, so give your postcard a personal touch by including family members or new friends in the scene. This card shows a different view of the château at Chenonceaux, with a rowing boat on the lake adding foreground interest. It was quickly and loosely sketched on the spot in pen and black ink, then watercolour washes were added later – a useful method of working if you don't want to take too many art materials out with you. The boat – the focal point of the scene – has been emphasized by the pink band around it.

4 ▾ Paint the water Take the ochre mix from step 3 down into the water to show the reflected façade of the château, but leave parts of the paper white to suggest reflected clouds. Mix a raw umber and cobalt blue wash and paint on to the water to represent the darker reflections. Leave to dry.

5 ◄ **Paint the roof**
Use a darker tone of the warm ochre mix to define the architectural details on the façade. Apply the same wash over the furthest tower. Mix cobalt blue and a touch of alizarin crimson watercolour for the slate roofs, taking some of the colour into the window openings.

6 ► **Add the trees**
The small clump of trees on the left is an important focus, drawing the eye through the painting. Apply touches of green oil pastel followed by a wash of raw umber and phthalo blue watercolour.

7 ▼ **Lay in the sky** Using the No. 12 brush, apply a dilute wash of cerulean blue watercolour across the sky – work loosely, leaving large patches of white for the clouds.

THE FINISHED PICTURE

A Paper clouds
In the sky area, most of the white paper was left unpainted to stand for the fluffy summer clouds.

B Economic marks
A dark wash, dabbed on with the tip of a No. 3 round brush, depicts with great economy window openings around the tower.

C Emphatic oil pastel
Streaks of black oil pastel were used to show reflections in the water. These opaque touches contrast with the transparent watercolour washes.

8 ▲ **Darken the roofs**
Use a No. 3 round brush and a mix of yellow ochre, alizarin crimson and raw umber to add more details to the building: the windows and the shadows down the sides of the towers. Using the cobalt blue/ alizarin crimson mix from step 5, add darker tones on the shaded roof areas.

The artist's garden

Look for inspiration in the landscape that is closest to home – your own garden. You can return to it time and time again and never exhaust its pictorial possibilities.

The pleasure of garden paintings lies in the intrinsic beauty of the subject, as well as the enjoyment of an individual artist's treatment of it. Gardening and art have been linked for thousands of years, initially in the regions where gardening began – Egypt and China. In more recent times, Claude Monet (1840–1926) painted his gardens at Argenteuil and Vétheuil in France many times, and in the 1890s moved to Giverny and began to plant his famous and much-painted water garden.

Exploiting your garden

A garden is an ideal subject, combining nature with man-made features. But the search for a 'picturesque' landscape can lead you to overlook this very obvious view right on your doorstep. It is convenient, accessible and offers plenty of opportunities to sketch, photograph, observe and become familiar with the subject. Record your garden at different times of day, in all weather conditions and in all seasons. In art, familiarity does not breed contempt. Indeed, it can give heightened awareness, and having an understanding of the subject allows you to develop creative interpretations. Returning to it time and again has a further benefit. Because you will have solved the basic problems first time around, you will be less concerned with pure description, which can be very liberating.

Gardens in watercolour

In this project the artist worked primarily from the three photos (left), but also from her memories of a garden that she created herself, has known intimately for many years and has painted many times. The photos were particularly useful for details – leaf shapes and patterns, the fall of light, the markings on the silver birch trunks and the objects on the table.

▶ **This fresh, light-filled painting was worked in transparent washes of watercolour. The artist painted quite slowly, building up patches of colour with a small brush.**

YOU WILL NEED

Piece of 300gsm (140lb) Not watercolour paper 57 x 38cm (22½ x 15in)

2B pencil or clutch pencil

11 watercolours: Van Dyke brown; sap green; ultramarine; lemon yellow; vermilion; alizarin crimson; cadmium yellow pale; burnt sienna; Winsor violet; purple madder; Winsor blue (green shade)

Brushes: Nos. 7 and 10 rounds; old toothbrush

White gouache

FIRST STEPS

1 ▼ **Establish the drawing** Using a 2B pencil or clutch pencil, start on the underdrawing. The subject is fairly complex, with a still life of dishes of fruit and a jug in the foreground, a wickerwork chair by the table and a complex mosaic of leaves in the background. Use the drawing to investigate and simplify leaf shapes and patterns of foliage.

2 ▼ **Lay the preliminary washes** The three vertical columns of the silver birch trunks are key elements of the composition. Use a mix of Van Dyke brown and sap green and a No. 7 round brush to paint the foliage behind the trunks, letting the negative spaces define the positive shapes of the trees. Paint clumps of leaves with the tip of the brush, adding ultramarine to the wash to vary the tones.

3 ▼ **Continue painting the foliage** Paint the sinuous shape of the tree in the background in Van Dyke brown. Develop the foliage, looking for the character and massed shapes of the leaves. Use the Van Dyke brown/sap green wash for this, modifying it with a little ultramarine for the cooler, bluer leaves.

4 ▶ **Work on the foreground** Dilute the Van Dyke brown/sap green/ultramarine wash and paint the glimpses of sky seen through the leaves. Paint the rest of the foliage with various mixes of these three colours, including the spiky leaves of the lily behind the wickerwork chair. Paint the lily flowers, using lemon yellow and wet-on-wet washes of vermilion/lemon yellow and alizarin crimson/cadmium yellow pale.

5 ▶ **Paint the wicker chair** Continue to work on the foliage behind the table, using variations of the Van Dyke brown/sap green/ultramarine wash. Add burnt sienna and Winsor violet for the darkest tones. Mix lemon yellow and Van Dyke brown to paint the chair – work carefully, avoiding flooding the paper with water. Paint the dark areas seen through the wickerwork in sap green and ultramarine.

6 ▶ **Add darker tones** With the tip of a No. 10 round brush, use a rich mix of Winsor violet, ultramarine and Van Dyke brown to paint the dark areas in the background and the shadows within the shrubs near the foreground. This will begin to create a sense of depth and form in the scene.

7 ▲ **Paint the jug** Switch back to the No. 7 round brush and paint the jug with separate washes of burnt sienna, Van Dyke brown and Winsor violet. Work wet-on-wet so that the colours bleed into each other, creating softly blended edges.

DEVELOPING THE PICTURE

Greens are a key component of this painting, and the range of light to dark and warm to cool greens has now been established. The next step is to work up some of the colourful features in the foreground, such as the brightly coloured cushion and the fruit.

8 ▼ **Work up the chair** Paint the patterned cushion on the chair, using a range of colours: vermilion, ultramarine, alizarin crimson, a mix of sap green and ultramarine, and a mix of lemon yellow and vermilion. Then paint the foliage around the chair, using your selection of green palette mixes. Fill in the holes in the wickerwork with the mix of sap green and ultramarine.

9 ▼ **Describe the apple** Paint the apple using the following washes applied wet-on-wet with the No. 10 round brush: lemon yellow, vermilion, sap green and a touch of Van Dyke brown. Allow the colours to blend softly.

10 ▼ **Colour the cherries** Paint the cherries, using alizarin crimson with a touch of lemon yellow. Add purple madder to the mix and apply to the shaded areas between the fruits – here you are using the negative spaces to define the shapes of the positive elements.

Express yourself
A different point of view

The artist has painted her garden – and the comfortable wicker chair – many times. In this study she has taken a different viewpoint, bringing the silver birch trees into the centre of the picture. She has stepped back so that a bank of white flowers fills the foreground and leads the eye into the scene. By changing your position you can create an entirely new image.

11 ▼ **Develop the 'still life'** Complete the cherries in the bowl with alizarin crimson, Winsor violet and purple madder, using Van Dyke brown for the stalks and ultramarine and Winsor blue for the bowl. Paint the second apple with lemon yellow, vermilion, sap green and a touch of Van Dyke brown. Add detail to the plate in ultramarine and Winsor blue, depicting the flower pattern and rim with a lemon yellow/vermilion mix. Finally, paint the scattered cherries with purple madder, alizarin crimson and lemon yellow.

12 ▼ **Continue with the foliage** Paint the foliage at top left with sap green and mixes of sap green with lemon yellow or ultramarine. Look for the areas of light and dark tone, the main part of the foliage and the particular leaf shapes such as those of the castor oil plant.

13 ▼ **Develop leaf shapes** Continue working down the left side of the painting, using the palest of your green washes to establish the leaf colours. Use the darker tones for the shadows that surround the leaves – these define the divided, finger-like outlines. Don't let the washes get too dry, as you need to establish the shapes but still keep the edges fairly soft.

EXPERT ADVICE
Head over heels

There are many reasons for turning your painting upside down. It helps you see the composition with fresh eyes, allowing you to focus on abstract areas of colour and tone without being distracted by the subject matter. Make any adjustments, then turn the painting back the right way up. There is also a practical reason for turning a large painting round. If you need to work on an area that is near the top edge, it is much easier to work with that edge nearest to you.

14 ◄ Add details on the tree trunks

Silver birches have a papery bark with dark horizontal and vertical markings. Use a sap green/Van Dyke brown mix applied with the tip of the No. 7 round brush to apply these markings.

15 ◄ Paint the pots

The warm tones and repeated ellipses of the terra-cotta pots behind the table are an important feature in this area of the painting. Paint them using burnt sienna, and a mix of burnt sienna with Van Dyke brown and touches of vermilion and lemon yellow.

16 ▶ **Paint the foliage** Apply a dilute ultramarine wash over the birch trunks to suggest their silvery tones. Using the negative/positive technique as in step 13, paint the lance-like leaves of the plant behind the jug. Begin by using sap green mixed with Winsor blue for the spaces between the leaves. Allow to dry a little, then apply a pale overall wash of sap green to colour the leaves themselves.

17 ▲ **Make some final adjustments** Apply washes of Van Dyke brown to the shaded sides of the birch trunks. Now work across the painting, making final adjustments. Use clean water to blend the colour and to soften any parts of the foliage that are too crisp and distracting.

A FEW STEPS FURTHER

You might want to carry the work further by adding some fine detail to the leaves and branches. Also, a spattering of white gouache will bring sparkling light into the painting.

18 ▲ **Apply body colour** Add white gouache to sap green watercolour and, using the No. 7 brush, add more fine, grass-like leaves in the foreground.

19 ▲ **Spatter colour** Load an old toothbrush with white gouache and spatter fine droplets of white to capture the effect of sparkling sunlight.

20 ▲ **Add cool shadows** Mix a fairly dilute wash of alizarin crimson and ultramarine, and apply purplish shadows with the No. 7 brush all over the tablecloth.

21 ▼ **Paint the branches** Mix Van Dyke brown with ultramarine and, using the tip of the brush, draw the dark tracery of branches. Work towards the tip, lifting the brush to create a line that tapers towards the end.

THE FINISHED PICTURE

A Defining negatives
Painting the dark shadows between the leaves of the castor oil plant allows the intricate indented shapes to emerge.

B Artistic licence
The artist altered the colour of the cushion on the chair so that it echoed the brighter colours of the items on the table.

C Paper whites
The white of the paper is important in watercolour – here it stands for the palest patches on the trunks of the silver birches.

Lively building site

It is not always the most picturesque scenes that provide the best subjects for the artist – urban and industrial landscapes have their own fascination.

The rather unusual subject matter in this project is matched by an equally unusual method of painting. Instead of working light to dark as you normally would with watercolours, start by laying in an area of dark tone to set a key for the picture. You can add the sky towards the end. Furthermore, try to approach the composition in a very direct way, applying a single layer of colour rather than building up layers of washes. Of course, this means you will have to judge and mix your colours accurately from the start, but the vibrant quality you will achieve – the white of the support glowing through a single layer of transparent colour – makes all your efforts worthwhile.

Using palette mixes

Some watercolour artists mix their colours in a very organized way, keeping each mix in a separate recess and washing their brush between each colour – an often recommended procedure. However, in keeping with your unusual approach, try working more intuitively instead, your brush dancing from one part of the palette to another.

As a result, the mixes will be gradually modified as touches of colour are blended inadvertently with those elsewhere on the palette. Inevitably they will begin to veer towards neutrals and coloured greys, the 'dirty' colours that you are sometimes warned against. In reality, these subtly modified mixes provide a range of ready-made tones that the artist can dip into. In any case, if you do not build up wash over wash, the colours retain their freshness.

With enough practice, this method can become second nature. You'll probably find that you can't tell precisely what your palette mixes consist of – just like a cook who adds a pinch of this and a bit of that to a recipe.

FIRST STROKES

1 ▶ **Make a pencil sketch** Sketch in the main elements of the composition with a B pencil. Work lightly, checking the balance of the components and the shapes they make on the paper.

2 ▼ **Start with the cab** Mix ultramarine, cerulean blue and emerald green. Using a 13mm (½in) flat brush, paint the back of the cab of the pile-driving rig. Load the brush with cadmium yellow and use the narrow edge of the brush to paint the warning stripes on the back. Use the flat edge to define the shape of the cab with a mix of cerulean blue, Prussian blue and burnt umber.

▲ The massive machine, the mounds of mud and earth, and the active, brightly clad workers were recorded in the artist's fluent, intuitive style of painting.

YOU WILL NEED

Piece of 300gsm (140lb) NOT watercolour paper 44 x 56cm (17 x 22in)

B pencil

15 watercolours: ultramarine; cerulean blue; emerald green; cadmium yellow; Prussian blue; burnt umber; raw umber; red ochre; cadmium orange; raw sienna; yellow ochre; cobalt blue; gold ochre; madder lake; violet

Brushes: 13mm (½in) and 10mm (⅜in) flats

Mixing palette

Calligraphy pen and white chalk

Narrow stick

Round-tipped painting knife

3 ▼ **Indicate dark tones** Block in the dark tones on the cab with a wash of raw umber, working wet-on-wet. Crisp up wet edges and draw in details with a calligraphy pen and the same wash. Sketch the head of the figure.

4 ▼ **Develop the rig** Block in the cab windows with the raw umber wash. Dip a narrow stick lengthways into the wash and apply the paint briskly to the paper to print the cables. Use the Prussian blue/cerulean mix and the 13mm (½in) brush to paint the jib (the arm of the crane) and pile-driver platform, then work into them with raw umber applied wet-on-wet.

5 ▲ **Add figures** Paint the pile-driving rod in red ochre, using the narrow edge of the 13mm (½in) brush. Hold the flat edge of the brush at an angle to the paper to mark the spiral of the auger. Block in the figures wet-on-wet. Use cadmium orange for the hats and the theodolite (a surveying instrument), cadmium yellow for the jackets, and a mix of Prussian blue and cadmium yellow for the trousers. The hat of the blue figure is emerald green, while his body is a pale version of the original blue wash from step 2.

6 ▶ **Block in the hoardings** Paint the hoardings with brush strokes of cadmium yellow, raw sienna and yellow ochre, applied wet-on-wet so that the colours run here and there. While the paint is still wet, pull a round-tipped painting knife across the wash in both directions, lifting the pigment to create highlights.

DEVELOPING THE PICTURE

Start to add details and fill in the background. Try to avoid overlaying the existing washes. The fewer layers of paint there are, the more vibrant the colours will be, so work background colours around existing shapes.

7 ▲ **Add detail** Use raw umber to print the crane and cables. Paint the rig tracks in cobalt blue, Prussian blue and raw umber. Apply foreground mixes of raw sienna, and yellow and gold ochres, using a 10mm (⅜in) brush. Mix burnt umber and Prussian blue for shadows on the auger. Put in the man on the right in emerald. Use madder lake with burnt umber for the red crane.

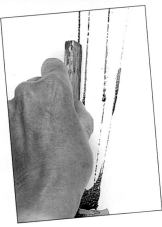

EXPERT ADVICE
Print-off techniques

If you draw complex patterns of cables too carefully, the result won't sit comfortably with a fluid watercolour style. Instead, print lines with a tool such as a stick or card. With this quick, direct technique, you are discouraged from overworking the painting.

8 ▲ **Add lettering** Using raw umber and raw sienna, block in the foreground and, while the paint is still wet, scrape into it with the painting knife. Mix a wash of red ochre and use the calligraphy pen to add struts to the crane boom, and lettering to the cab of the rig.

9 ◄ **Define the figures** Add a few defining marks to the figures with freely drawn lines made with the dip pen and red ochre mixed with burnt umber – these pull the loosely rendered figures into focus. Change back to the 13mm (½in) brush and indicate the buildings in the background with a cool grey from your palette. Add the dark figure in the foreground using burnt umber with some of your palette mixes, then use a warm, neutral palette mix to fill in the gaps between the figures.

Express yourself

Heavy machinery

This is another of the artist's vigorous watercolours, inspired by a visit to the same building site. When you have worked through this project, why not find a similar site and make some sketches on the spot? While the experience is still fresh in your mind, work up a watercolour, using the direct, single-layer approach illustrated in the step-by-step.

10 ◄ **Add the sky** Wet the upper part of the painting by flooding it with water under a tap, then dot in violet and ultramarine. Lift and tilt the paper to make the colour run and blend to create a graduated sky. The accidental softening of colours in adjacent areas, such as the pile driver and some of the figures, gives the painting a sense of fluidity and spontaneity.

11 ▲ **Add crisp details** Having softened some of the edges, pull the image into focus again by adding fine detail. Use pen and a brown palette mix to add a sketchy outline to the dark foreground figure – the crisp lines give the image a sense of movement. Use the pen to draw the rope in the foreground and the crane booms in the distance.

12 ▲ **Add texture in the foreground** Using the dark brown mix from your palette, add gestural marks to the disturbed ground in the foreground. This creates visual interest and provides a link with dark areas elsewhere in the painting.

A FEW STEPS FURTHER

There is now a convincing sense of noise, dust, and hustle and bustle in the painting. Decide whether you want to add more detail in the foreground – this will bring the area forward and increase the illusion of depth.

14 ▲ **Add highlights** Use white chalk to add a few sparkling highlights – on the edges of the auger, on the back of the dark jacket and on the ground. These highlights should be used sparingly and applied lightly, so that the stick glances over the dimpled surface of the paper to give a stippled effect.

13 ▲ **Spatter the foreground** Mix a wash of cadmium orange and use this to spatter the foreground, adding lively texture here.

THE FINISHED PICTURE

A One layer
Subtle areas of mixed colour, applied as a single layer, give the paint surface a sparkling, jewel-like brilliance and clarity.

B Foreground texture
Gestural marks and spattering create visually entertaining passages in the foreground. The large scale of the marks here helps to suggest recession from foreground to background.

C Lost and found
Edges that have been 'lost' by washing off, then 'found' with a pen line produce figures that have an appealing immediacy and sense of movement.

Tree-lined road

Transform a bleak, monochromatic winter scene into a warm, atmospheric watercolour by adding a little sunshine and touches of colourful autumn foliage.

The two stately trees dramatically outlined against the sky are a major feature of this village scene. The reference photograph was taken in the winter – a good time for artists to study trees, as, devoid of foliage, their shape, structure and proportions are easier to see. What you learn from painting winter trees will reap rewards when you come to paint trees in summer and autumn.

With his long experience of observing and painting trees, the artist felt free to add some clumps of autumn foliage to the bare winter ones in the photo to give them added colour and interest. By using warm colours throughout and adding a blue sky, the artist has created a lively interpretation of the subject.

To enliven further the colours and emphasize the contrast, the artist added sunlight to the overcast scene. In the painting, the sun is low and off to the right, throwing long shadows across the road. It also brings out the cylindrical form of the trees and the angular form of the cottage.

Using a rigger brush

The branches of the trees were painted with a rigger brush. This has extra-long hairs and can make very expressive marks. If you've never used one, make some practice strokes first to learn how to control the brush.

Try sketching some simple trees. Hold the brush near the ferrule to make small marks, but, if you want to exploit the flexibility of the brush for creating elegant, tapering lines, hold it lightly, nearer the end of the handle. Keep your hand still and move the brush with your fingers, letting the long hairs twist and bend to make delicate strokes.

▼ **Warm, sunlit areas contrast with cooler shadows and an expanse of blue sky in this picturesque study of a tree-lined road.**

Piece of 300gsm (140lb) rough watercolour paper 30 x 42cm (11½ x 16½in)

4B pencil

7 watercolours: raw sienna; cadmium red; ultramarine; cobalt blue; light red; lemon yellow; burnt sienna

Brushes: 38mm (1½in) and 19mm (¾in) flats; Nos. 14 and 6 rounds; No. 1 rigger

Mixing palette or dish

Jar of water

Ruler

FIRST STEPS

1 ► Sketch the scene
Using a 4B pencil, make an outline drawing of the scene. You might find it helpful to mark the horizon line lightly and visualize the lines of the cottage roof and walls receding to the vanishing point. Feel free to omit ugly details such as the street light and road markings.

2 ◄ Lay down the initial wash
Tilt up your board slightly. Using a 38mm (1½in) flat brush, dampen the paper, except for the cottage area, with clean water. Change to a 19mm (¾in) flat and mix a pale wash of raw sienna – make the colour a little stronger than you need, as it will dilute on the damp surface of the paper. Brush the wash across the lower part of the sky and the foreground.

3 ▼ Add warmth to the sky While the paper is still just damp, sweep a band of thinly diluted cadmium red across the lower sky, just above the band of raw sienna. Allow it to melt softly into the raw sienna to give a touch of autumnal afternoon warmth.

DEVELOPING THE PICTURE

These initial blushes of colour will establish the overall warm tonality of the scene, as they will glow through the overlaid washes of colour to come.

4 ▲ Paint the upper sky Mix a wash of ultramarine and a little cobalt blue. Still using the 19mm (¾in) flat brush, sweep this across the upper sky, letting the colour drift gently down the damp paper in a graduated wash.

5 ▶ Finish the sky
Lighten the wash with more water as you work down the paper. Make flicking diagonal strokes at the edges of the picture to give some movement to the sky (as long as the paper is still damp, these will dry as soft shapes). Leave the mid-section of the sky untouched.

6 ▲ Block in the background Use some of the ultramarine sky colour to make an underwash for the line of trees glimpsed in the far distance. Make a series of short, vertical strokes with the tip of the brush.

7 ▼ Underpaint the trees Lightly place a few broad, vertical strokes of burnt sienna around the tops of the trees, keeping the brush almost dry. Pick up a little more raw sienna on the brush tip and paint the tree trunks with short, horizontal strokes.

8 ▶ **Paint the cottage roof** Add some cadmium red to the raw sienna on your palette to warm it. Change to a No. 14 round brush and paint the roofs of the cottage, leaving flecks of white paper to stand for the branches of the small tree on the right.

9 ▼ **Paint the chimneys** Darken the mix slightly with a hint of ultramarine and, using a No. 6 round brush, paint the chimneys and chimney pots. Leave slivers of bare paper for the flashing at the top and base of the chimneys.

10 ▲ **Put in the windows** Use a very dilute mix of ultramarine and cobalt blue to show the sky reflected in the window panes, varying the tone to suggest light and shadow. Leave the glazing bars white, but blur them slightly so that they are not over-defined.

11 ◀ **Paint the garden wall** Mix together cadmium red, light red and a touch of ultramarine to make a slightly cooler red than that used on the roof. Paint the garden wall with the tip of the No. 14 round brush, leaving flecks of white here and there. Paint around the posts in the foreground. Mix a green from lemon yellow and ultramarine, and use this to suggest moss and foliage growing on the wall.

12 ▶ **Return to the trees** Mix lemon yellow and a little raw sienna to make a light, warm yellow. With the No. 6 round brush, start to define the main clumps of foliage on the tall trees. Hold the brush almost parallel with the paper and work it with a sideways motion, letting the colour break up on the textured surface of the paper.

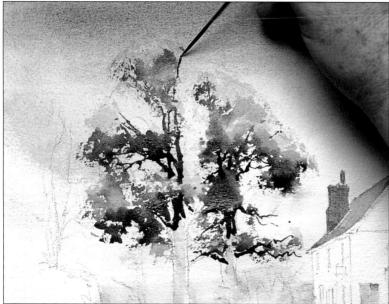

13 ▼ **Paint dark foliage** Add more raw sienna and some ultramarine to the wash. Put in the dark green clumps of foliage, again laying the brush almost flat to the paper and skipping it lightly across the surface with a sideways motion to make broken-edged marks, as before.

14 ◀ **Paint the branches** Use broken strokes of burnt sienna to suggest clumps of brown leaves, letting the colour blur into the green. Mix a near-black from ultramarine, raw sienna and light red, and paint the branches with a No. 1 rigger brush. Start at the trunk and pull the brush in the direction of growth, skipping in and out of the foliage clumps. Vary the pressure on the brush to make the lines swell and taper.

Express yourself
Pen and colour wash

This country scene has a similar composition to the one in the step-by-step. The curve of the road leads the eye into the picture and tall trees dominate the sky area. This time the scene is worked up in more detail. The initial line drawing is made with a dip pen and waterproof Indian ink and is then washed over with watercolour. The ink lines give structure to the image and sharpen up architectural features, while the freely applied washes create a fresh, lively feel. The pen has been used in a similar way to the rigger brush to suggest the tree branches.

15 ▶ **Put in distant trees** With the No. 6 round brush, model the tree trunks by painting their shadowed sides with a mix of ultramarine and light red (see Expert Advice, right). Suggest the slanting shadows cast on to the trunks by the branches. Paint the more distant trees with varied mixes of ultramarine and light red, leaving a broken glimmer of white paper along the top of the wall.

EXPERT ADVICE
Modelling the trunks

To suggest the cylindrical form of the tree trunks, first dampen them with water, then put in the shadow colour down one edge with a slightly wavering vertical stroke. The colour will fade out softly on the damp surface, creating a tonal graduation from dark to light.

16 ◀ **Work on the foreground** Use the same colours and techniques as for the two main trees to paint the foliage and grass on the left (paint these slightly more freely – elements on the edges of the image should be understated, so as not to compete with the centre of interest). Mix lemon yellow with a touch of ultramarine and paint the grass verge on the right with loose strokes of the No. 14 brush.

17 ▲ **Model the cottage** Suggest the kerb with light red and ultramarine. Mix a dilute wash of ultramarine and a hint of light red. Using the No. 6 brush, paint shadows on the brick wall, roofs and chimneys. Clean your brush, then put in the shadows on the cottage.

18 ▲ **Add cast shadows** Indicate the kerb on the left with curved strokes of raw sienna greyed with ultramarine. Leave to dry, then use the ultramarine/light red mix to put in the shadows cast across the road by the small tree on the right. Darken the mix slightly for the broken shadow in the immediate foreground, cast by unseen trees to the right.

A FEW STEPS FURTHER

The picture is almost complete, the contrast of warm and cool colours capturing the atmosphere of a crisp, bright autumn day. All that remains is to bring in a few dark details to give the image a bit of punch.

19 ▼ **Finish painting the cottage** Paint the barge boards at the gable end of the cottage with the ultramarine/light red mix. Steady the brush by resting the ferrule on the edge of a ruler held at an angle to the paper.

20 ▲ **Paint the small tree** Use the rigger brush and mixes of raw sienna and ultramarine to put in dark reflections in the cottage windows and to paint the small tree on the right. Vary the tones to evoke the play of light and shadow on the trunk and branches. Skip the brush lightly over the paper to suggest finer branches.

THE FINISHED PICTURE

A Calligraphic strokes
The fine rigger brush makes expressive strokes that suggest the gnarled and twisted forms of the branches.

B Stable design
Both the horizon line and the tallest tree have been positioned according to the 'rule of thirds', creating a balanced composition.

C Foreground shadows
The blue-grey shadows cast by unseen trees in the foreground help to 'frame' the scene along the bottom edge.